The Academy of Television
Arts & Sciences
Welcomes You
to the 1997 Annual
Emmy Awards
for
Nighttime Programming

1

THANK YOU, ATAS,
CONGRATULATIONS TO ALL

THE LARRY SANDERS SHOW
STARRING GARRY SHANDLING

Comedy Series

Lead Actor in a Comedy Series
Garry Shandling

Supporting Actor in a Comedy Series
Jeffrey Tambor

Supporting Actor in a Comedy Series
Rip Torn

Supporting Actress in a Comedy Series
Janeane Garofalo

Directing for a Comedy Series
"Ellen, Or Isn't She?"
Alan Myerson

Directing for a Comedy Series
"Everybody Loves Larry"
Todd Holland

Writing for a Comedy Series
"Ellen, Or Isn't She?"
Judd Apatow, John Markus, Teleplay/Story;
Garry Shandling, Story

Writing for a Comedy Series
"Everybody Loves Larry"
Jon Vitti

Writing for a Comedy Series
"My Name Is Asher Kingsley"
Peter Tolan

Guest Actor in a Comedy Series
David Duchovny

Guest Actress in a Comedy Series
Ellen DeGeneres

Multi-Camera Picture Editing for a Series (2)

Lighting Direction (Electronic)
for a Comedy Series

Sound Mixing for a Comedy Series or a Special

MISS EVERS' BOYS

Made for Television Movie
The President's Award

Lead Actor in a Miniseries or a Special
Laurence Fishburne

Lead Actress in a Miniseries or a Special
Alfre Woodard

Supporting Actor in a Miniseries or a Special
Obba Babatundé

Supporting Actor in a Miniseries or a Special
Ossie Davis

Writing for a Miniseries or a Special
Walter Bernstein, Teleplay

Casting for a Miniseries or a Special

Choreography

Cinematography for a Miniseries or a Special

Single-Camera Picture Editing for a Miniseries
or a Special

Makeup for a Miniseries or a Special

IF THESE WALLS COULD TALK

Made for Television Movie
The President's Award

Single-Camera Picture Editing for a Miniseries
or a Special

Hairstyling for a Miniseries or a Special

DENNIS MILLER LIVE

Variety, Music or Comedy Series

Writing for a Variety or Music Program
Eddie Feldmann, Supervising Writer;
Dennis Miller, David Feldman, Mike Gandolfi,
Tom Hertz, Rick Overton, Leah Krinsky,
Jim Hanna, Writers

BETTE MIDLER:
DIVA LAS VEGAS

Variety, Music or Comedy Special

Performance in a Variety or Music Program
Bette Midler

Directing for a Variety or Music Program
Marty Callner

Music Direction

Art Direction for a Variety or Music Program

Costume Design for a Variety or Music Program

Multi-Camera Picture Editing for a Miniseries
or a Special

Hairstyling for a Miniseries or a Special

Lighting Direction (Electronic) for a
Drama Series, Variety Series, Miniseries
or a Special

Sound Mixing for a Variety or Music Series
or a Special

CRIME OF THE CENTURY

Directing for a Miniseries or a Special
Mark Rydell

Writing for a Miniseries or a Special
William Nicholson

Casting for a Miniseries or a Special

Single-Camera Picture Editing for a Miniseries
or a Special

GEORGE CARLIN:
40 YEARS OF COMEDY

Variety, Music or Comedy Special

Performance in a Variety or Music Program
George Carlin

THANKS TO THE ATAS BOARD OF GOVERNORS FOR
THE 1997 GOVERNORS AWARD FOR A DECADE OF "COMIC RELIEF.™"

FOR 90 NOMINATIONS!
OUR EMMY® AWARD NOMINEES!

TRACEY TAKES ON...
Variety, Music or Comedy Series

Performance in a Variety or Music Program
Tracey Ullman

Writing for a Variety or Music Program
Tracey Ullman, Jerry Belson, Dick Clement,
Ian La Frenais, Allen J. Zipper, Robert Klane,
Jenji Kohan, Molly Newman,
Gail Parent, Writers

Directing for a Variety or Music Program
"1976"
Thomas Schlamme

Art Direction for a Variety or Music Program

Costume Design for a Variety or Music Program

Hairstyling for a Series

Makeup for a Series

WEAPONS OF MASS DISTRACTION
Writing for a Miniseries or a Special
Larry Gelbart

Art Direction for a Miniseries or a Special

Casting for a Miniseries or a Special

Sound Mixing for a Drama, Miniseries
or a Special

GRAND AVENUE
Casting for a Miniseries or a Special

TAXICAB CONFESSIONS III
Informational Special

THE CHEROKEE KID
Sound Editing for a Miniseries or a Special

GOTTI
Made for Television Movie

Lead Actor in a Miniseries or a Special
Armand Assante

Directing for a Miniseries or a Special
Robert Harmon

Writing for a Miniseries or a Special
Steve Shagan

Cinematography for a Miniseries or a Special

Single-Camera Picture Editing for a Miniseries
or a Special

Sound Mixing for a Drama, Miniseries
or a Special

PARADISE LOST: THE CHILD MURDERS AT ROBIN HOOD HILLS
Informational Special

Achievement in Informational Programming —
Cinematography

Achievement in Informational Programming —
Picture Editing

MEMPHIS PD: WAR ON THE STREETS
Achievement in Informational Programming —
Picture Editing

WITHOUT PITY: A FILM ABOUT ABILITIES
Informational Special

Achievement in Informational Programming —
Picture Editing

IN THE GLOAMING
Made for Television Movie

Lead Actress in a Miniseries or a Special
Glenn Close

Supporting Actress in a Miniseries or a Special
Bridget Fonda

Directing for a Miniseries or a Special
Christopher Reeve

Cinematography for a Miniseries or a Special

CHRIS ROCK: BRING THE PAIN
Variety, Music or Comedy Special

Writing for a Variety or Music Program
Chris Rock

THE SECOND CIVIL WAR
Supporting Actor in a Miniseries or a Special
Beau Bridges

HOW DO YOU SPELL GOD?
Children's Program

Achievement in Informational Programming —
Picture Editing

SMOKE ALARM: THE UNFILTERED TRUTH ABOUT CIGARETTES
Children's Program

TALKED TO DEATH
Informational Special

http://www.hbo.com

WELCOME HOME.

WE ARE PROUD TO HOST THIS YEAR'S EMMY® AWARDS
AND CONGRATULATE ALL OF TONIGHT'S WINNERS AND NOMINEES.

Contents

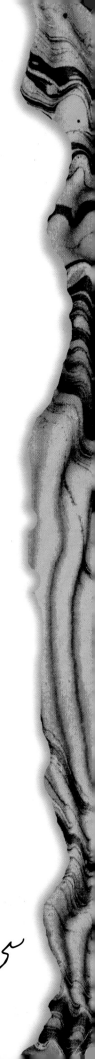

PARAMOUNT
CONGRATULATES
THE 1996-97
EMMY NOMINEES

President's Message

Next month I'll be turning my gavel over to a new Television Academy president. During my six years as president and 13 years serving in various positions as an Academy officer and committee chairman, I have had the pleasure to work with many talented and dedicated ATAS officers, governors, staffers and members. Together we have helped the Academy achieve its status as the largest and most influential organization engaged in the arts and sciences of national television. So it is with pride that I consider some of the milestones reached by the Academy during my tenure.

ATAS has a balanced budget and, fiscally, is healthier than it has ever been. This is reflected in the year-round administration of the Primetime and Daytime Emmy Awards, the increased the number of activities for Academy members, ATAS's many educational services, the publishing of *Emmy* magazine, the maintaining of the ATAS Hall of Fame and the recent establishment of the Archive of American Television.

The Academy purchased the Leonard H. Goldenson Theatre and Conference Centre, further establishing ATAS headquarters as a center for industry activity. And ATAS has an ideal arrangement for its main office building — a 50-year, no-cost lease.

The Primetime Emmys returned to an annual rotation among the major broadcast networks. This year's telecast marks a return to CBS after a 10-year hiatus; next year the 50th Annual Emmy Awards will be seen on NBC. Since 1986 the license fees for the program have more than doubled.

The Academy presented the Superhighway Summit at UCLA, still regarded as one of the industry's most distinguished conferences on new media. Vice President Al Gore participated, along with the top executives in telecommunications. Many in our business credit the summit as the wake-up call for the next generation of this industry.

And ATAS produced an animated half-hour program about the dangers of substance abuse that was aired simultaneously by all of the broadcast networks. *Cartoon All-Stars to the Rescue* also was aired extensively by independent stations and cable networks and was lauded by a joint session of Congress and many key anti–substance abuse organizations, including the Partnership for a Drug Free America, for helping to change children's views about drugs.

I feel good about these and numerous other Academy accomplishments. I will relinquish the gavel next month with the satisfaction of knowing that the Academy holds an important place in the fast-moving world of telecommunications.

I am grateful to have had the honor of serving you. I extend my warm congratulations to all of the Primetime Emmy nominees and winners.

Richard H. Frank
President, Academy of Television Arts & Sciences

Emmy Interregnum

By Libby Slate

Tonight's *49th Annual Primetime Emmy Awards* presentation serves as a bridge between two milestones: last year's observance of the Television Academy's 50th Anniversary, and next year's celebration of the 50th Annual Primetime Emmy Awards ceremony.

maximum amount of people," Loper adds. "That leads into the 50th Anniversary of the Emmys. But this year's ceremony stands on its own. Hopefully, it will be very successful."

That first Emmy ceremony back on January 25, 1949, may pale in comparison to tonight's star-

"In government, they would call that the interregnum," says ATAS Executive Director Dr. James L. Loper. "That's the time when the President has been elected, but not sworn in. You finish one thing, and you look forward to the next. I can only imagine what was going through the minds of our founders between the time they established the Academy and presented the first Emmy Awards.

"We felt that the 50th Anniversary celebration of the Academy was very successful, with the number of different programs, which reached the

studded gala, but it was a gala nevertheless. Banners festooned the old Hollywood Athletic Club on Sunset Boulevard, where six Emmy Awards were bestowed, and searchlights illuminated the sky. The tickets cost only $5.00 but, true to the some-things-never-change spirit, they were sold out long before the show.

The awards moved to the Ambassador Hotel the following year, where they remained through 1952, taking place at the famed Cocoanut Grove. In 1953 the ceremony was moved to the Statler

Continued on page 10

8

Movies

Television

Books

Music

Video

Multimedia

All moving,
all changing,
often converging.

Unscramble the signals.
Connect the dots.
Get the picture.

Don't miss a beat.

Sometimes we wish there were an Emmy® for watching TV.

Entertainment WEEKLY
On the pulse of popular culture.

Continued from page 8

Hotel, and in 1954 — the only year the show was not televised — changed again, to the Hollywood Palladium.

On March 7, 1955, two ceremonies took place simultaneously — at the Moulin Rouge night club in Hollywood and Nino's LaRue restaurant in New York City, reflecting the growing involvement of the New York television community with the Academy and foreshadowing the establishment later that year of a separate New York chapter. The shows were broadcast nationally for the first time with NBC doing the honors. Two concurrent presentations were made each year through 1958; that year's 10th anniversary event was also the first after the 1957 creation of the New York-based National Academy of Television Arts and Sciences.

In 1959, no less than three Emmy ceremonies were held simultaneously, at the Moulin Rouge in Hollywood, Ziegfeld Theatre in New York, and Mayflower Hotel in Washington, D.C. For the next two years, only Los Angeles and New York did the honors, but our nation's capital chimed back in 1962 and 1963. The 1964 presentations took place at the Hollywood Palladium and the Music Hall of the Texas pavilion at the New York World's Fair. Other notable sites of the two-city ceremonies, which continued through 1970, include the Century Plaza Hotel in 1967 and the Santa Monica Civic Auditorium and Carnegie Hall, both in 1969, with Carnegie repeating in 1970.

The sole Emmy site in 1971 and 1972 was the Hollywood Palladium. In 1973, the News and Documentary awards were held separately for the first time, at the New York Hilton Hotel, two days after the Entertainment awards ceremony at the Shubert Theatre in Los Angeles. In 1974, the first-ever Daytime Emmy Awards were telecast in a Rockefeller Plaza ceremony, with the re-christened Primetime Awards bestowed at the Pantages Theatre in Hollywood and the News and Documentary statuettes at the New York Hilton. Neither of the latter categories was awarded in 1975, while the Primetime

ceremony returned to the Hollywood Palladium. In 1976, the first separate Creative Arts ceremony was held at the Beverly Wilshire Hotel in Beverly Hills.

The year 1977 proved historic in Emmy annals, chiefly because of the Television Academy's reorganization. The newly re-established Academy of Television Arts and Sciences in Los Angeles took over the presentation of the Primetime entertainment awards, while NATAS continued to supervise Daytime, Sports and the newly reinstated News and Documentary awards. Also, the ATAS ceremony was staged for the first time at the Pasadena Civic Auditorium, where it has been presented every year since.

Attendees of this year's Emmy Creative Arts and Primetime honors will be the first to enjoy the Pasadena Civic's new look, as the 67-year-old building completed a $1.4-million renovation and restoration on September 1. The familiar red-and-white seating color scheme has been replaced with the original teal blue and dark brown, according to Pasadena Civic Auditorium General Manager Richard Barr; and there is more seating for people with disabilities. The lobby is brighter, its original brass and pewter wall sconces restored. The restrooms have marble-topped sinks and counters instead of porcelain and their capacity has been doubled, while there are now handicapped restroom facilities accessible by a newly re-worked elevator.

"I think people are going to be more comfortable," says Barr, who worked with the architectural firm Miralles and Associates in coordination with the City of Pasadena's Cultural Planning Commission, as the building is listed with the National Register of Historic Places. "The surroundings are very elegant and special. They will add to the glamour of the occasion."

This year's occasion is the next to last in the broadcasting rotation of the Big Four networks. Executive director Loper says that within the next year a committee will form to negotiate a new wheel. He foresees no major problems; after all, he says, the current wheel "worked out just fine."

Congratulations to all the Emmy® nominees and winners on their outstanding work.

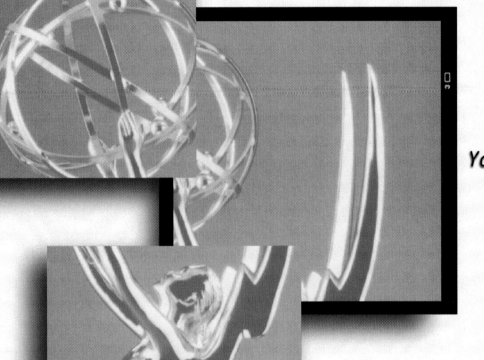

Your talent inspires.

Your work challenges.

Your efforts are recognized.

www.showtimeonline.com

must see

ER

Outstanding Drama Series
Constant c Productions, Amblin Television in association with Warner Bros. Television

The President's Award
Constant c Productions, Amblin Television in association with Warner Bros. Television

Outstanding Lead Actor In A Drama Series
Anthony Edwards as Dr. Mark Greene

Outstanding Lead Actress In A Drama Series
Julianna Margulies as Carol Hathaway

Outstanding Lead Actress In A Drama Series
Sherry Stringfield as Dr. Susan Lewis

Outstanding Supporting Actor In A Drama Series
Eriq LaSalle as Dr. Peter Benton

Outstanding Supporting Actor In A Drama Series
Noah Wyle as Dr. John Carter

Outstanding Supporting Actress In A Drama Series
Laura Innes as Dr. Kerry Weaver

Outstanding Supporting Actress In A Drama Series
CCH Pounder as Dr. Angela Hicks

Outstanding Supporting Actress In A Drama Series
Gloria Reuben as Jeanie Boulet

Outstanding Guest Actor In A Drama Series
William H. Macy as Dr. Morgenstern

Outstanding Guest Actor In A Drama Series
Ewan McGregor as Duncan Stewart

Outstanding Guest Actress In A Drama Series
Veronica Cartwright as Norma

Outstanding Directing For A Drama Series
Tom Moore, *Union Station*

Outstanding Directing For A Drama Series
Rod Holcomb, *Last Call*

Outstanding Directing For A Drama Series
Christopher Chulack, *Fear Of Flying*

Outstanding Writing For A Drama Series
John Wells, *Faith*

Outstanding Writing For A Drama Series
Neal Baer, *Whose Appy Now?*

Outstanding Single-Camera Picture Editing For A Series
Kevin Casey, *Union Station*

Outstanding Single-Camera Picture Editing For A Series
Randy Jon Morgan, *The Long Way Around*

Outstanding Casting For A Series
John Levey, Barbara Miller

Outstanding Sound Mixing For A Drama Series
Lowell Harris, Allen L. Stone, Frank Jones, Michael E. Jiron, *Fear Of Flying*

Seinfeld

Outstanding Comedy Series
Castle Rock Entertainment

Outstanding Supporting Actor In A Comedy Series
Jason Alexander as George Costanza

Outstanding Supporting Actor In A Comedy Series
Michael Richards as Kramer

Outstanding Supporting Actress In A Comedy Series
Julia Louis-Dreyfus as Elaine Benes

Outstanding Guest Actor In A Comedy Series
Jerry Stiller as Frank Costanza

Outstanding Directing For A Comedy Series
Andy Ackerman, *The Pothole*

Outstanding Writing For A Comedy Series
Peter Mehlman, Jill Franklyn, *The Yada Yada*

Outstanding Multi-Camera Picture Editing For A Series
Skip Collector, *The Pothole*

Outstanding Casting For A Series
Marc Hirschfeld, Meg Liberman, Brian Myers

Mad About You

Outstanding Comedy Series
Infront Productions and Nuance Productions in association with TriStar Television

Outstanding Lead Actor In A Comedy Series
Paul Reiser as Paul Buchman

Outstanding Lead Actress In A Comedy Series
Helen Hunt as Jamie Buchman

Outstanding Guest Actor In A Comedy Series
Mel Brooks as Uncle Phil

Outstanding Guest Actor In A Comedy Series
Sid Caesar as Harold

Outstanding Guest Actress In A Comedy Series
Carol Burnett as Teresa

Suddenly Susan

Outstanding Guest Actress In A Comedy Series
Betty White as Midge Haber

NewsRadio

Outstanding Costuming For A Series
Luellyn Harper, *Awards Show*

Frasier

Outstanding Comedy Series
Grub Street Productions in association with Paramount Network Television

Outstanding Lead Actor In A Comedy Series
Kelsey Grammer as Dr. Frasier Crane

Outstanding Supporting Actor In A Comedy Series
David Hyde Pierce as Dr. Niles Crane

Outstanding Guest Actor In A Comedy Series
James Earl Jones as Norman

Outstanding Guest Actress In A Comedy Series
Marsha Mason as Sherry

Outstanding Directing For A Comedy Series
David Lee, *To Kill A Talking Bird*

Outstanding Multi-Camera Picture Editing For A Series
Ron Volk, *To Kill A Talking Bird*

Outstanding Casting For A Series
Jeff Greenberg

Outstanding Sound Mixing For A Comedy Series Or A Special
Dana Mark McClure, John Reiner, Andre Caporaso, Robert Douglass, *Liar, Liar!*

3rd Rock from the Sun

Outstanding Comedy Series
Carsey-Werner Productions, LLC

Outstanding Lead Actor In A Comedy Series
John Lithgow as Dick Solomon

Outstanding Supporting Actress In A Comedy Series
Kristen Johnston as Sally Solomon

Outstanding Choreography
Marguerite Derricks, *A Nightmare On Dick Street*

Outstanding Costume Design For A Series
Melina Root, *A Nightmare On Dick Street*

Outstanding Hairstyling For A Series
Pixie Schwartz, *A Nightmare On Dick Street*

Outstanding Sound Mixing For A Comedy Series Or A Special
Jesse Peck, Todd Grace, Craig Porter, *A Nightmare on Dick Street*

Friends

Outstanding Supporting Actress In A Comedy Series
Lisa Kudrow as Phoebe Buffay

nominees!

Law & Order

Outstanding Drama Series
Wolf Films in association with Universal Television

Outstanding Lead Actor In A Drama Series
Sam Waterston as Assistant D.A. Jack McCoy

Outstanding Cinematography For A Series
Constantine Makris, *Mad Dog*

Outstanding Single-Camera Picture Editing For A Series
David Siegel, *Judgement In L.A., Part 2*

Outstanding Sound Mixing For A Drama Series
**David Platt, William M. Nicholson,
Thomas Meloeny,** *D-Girl*

Homicide: Life on the Street

Outstanding Guest Actress In A Drama Series
Anne Meara as Donna DiGrazi

Outstanding Casting For A Series
Lou Digiamo, Pat Moran

Profiler

Outstanding Sound Editing For A Series
**Peter Austin, Michael Thomas Babcock,
Linda Keim, Kenneth Johnson, Paul Longstaffe,
Warren Smith, Kim Naves,** *Cruel and Unusual*

Crisis Center

Outstanding Main Title Theme Music
Danny Lux

Dark Skies

Outstanding Main Title Design
Mike Jones

Outstanding Main Title Theme Music
Michael Hoenig

The Tonight Show with Jay Leno

Outstanding Variety, Music Or Comedy Series
**Big Dog Productions in association with
NBC Studios, Inc.
Debbie Vickers,** Executive Producer; **Patti Grant,**
Supervising Producer; **Larry Goitia,** Line Producer;
Jay Leno, Producer

Outstanding Directing For A Variety Or Music Program
Ellen Brown *Show #1062*

Outstanding Lighting Direction (Electronic) For A Drama
Series, Variety Series, Miniseries Or A Special
Gary Thorns

Outstanding Technical Direction/Camera/Video For A Series
**Michael Stramisky, Les Atkinson, Hank Geving,
Rob Palmer, Kurt Tonnessen, Kevin Fraser,
Bill Gardhouse, Jr.,** *Show #1079*

Late Night With Conan O'Brien 3rd Anniversary Show

Outstanding Writing For A Variety Or Music Program
**Jonathan Groff, Tom Agna, Chris Albers,
Tommy Blacha, Greg Cohen, Janine DiTullio,
Michael Gordon, Brian Kiley, Ellie Barancik,
Brian McCann, Conan O'Brien, Brian Reich,
Andy Richter, Mike Sweeney, Robert Smigel**

Saturday Night Live

Outstanding Technical Direction/Camera/Video For A Series
**Steven Cimino, Jan Kasoff, Michael Bennett,
Carl Eckett, John Pinto, Robert Reese, Gregory Aull,
Frank Grisanti,** *Hosted by Dana Carvey And
Musical Guest Dr. Dre*

National Geographic Special: Tigers of the Snow

Outstanding Informational Special
**National Geographic Television
Nicolas Noxon,** Executive Producer; **Mark Stouffer,**
Producer/Director; **Kevin McCarey,** Writer

Outstanding Achievement In Informational Programming
Bill Mills, Director of Photography

Outstanding Achievement In Informational Programming
Barry Nye, A.C.E., Editor

Outstanding Achievement In Informational Programming
Barry Nye, A.C.E., Sound Editor

Outstanding Achievement In Informational Programming
Paul Trautman, Production Mixer; **Paul Schremp,
Darren Barnett, Pattie Lorusso,** Re-Recording Mixers

The Odyssey

Outstanding Miniseries
**Hallmark Entertainment in association with
American Zoetrope**

Outstanding Directing For A Miniseries Or A Special
Andrei Konchalovsky, *Part I & II*

Outstanding Art Direction For A Miniseries Or A Special
**Roger Hall, John King, Frederic Evard,
Karen Brookes** *Part II*

Outstanding Hairstyling For A Miniseries Or A Special
Suzanne Stokes-Munton, Petra Schaumann

Centennial Olympic Games: Opening Ceremonies

Outstanding Directing For A Variety Or Music Program
Don Mischer

Outstanding Art Direction For A Variety Or Music Program
Bob Keene, Steve Bass

Outstanding Music Direction
Mark Watters

Outstanding Music And Lyrics
**David Foster, Kenneth "Babyface" Edmonds,
Linda Thompson,** *"The Power Of The Dream"*

Outstanding Music And Lyrics
Mark Watters, Lorraine Feather,
"Faster, Higher, Stronger"

Outstanding Lighting Direction (Electronic) For A Drama
Series, Variety Series, Miniseries Or A Special
**John C. Morgan, Robert Barnhart,
Robert A. Dickinson**

Outstanding Sound Mixing For A Variety Or Music Series
Or A Special
Edward J. Greene

**We proudly thank the talented individuals
who've made the past year a winning season for us,
for television, and for viewers.**

Last year, the AMC documentary *Blacklist: Hollywood on Trial* became the first winner of the newly inaugurated President's Award, an Emmy Award conceived in response to the unfounded political criticism that television presents an abundance of irresponsible programming.

The award honors a program that illuminates a social or educational issue and in the process, encourages society to deal with and change that particular situation. Presented to the network, production company and studio, it is voted upon by the Academy Board of Governors rather than by the Peer Panels of most other Emmy category finalists. Any program otherwise eligible for a Primetime Emmy is eligible for the President's Award, the only circumstance under which the same program can win twice, for its basic category and for this award.

This year's five nominees are:

A&E *Biography* , a repeat nominee, which A&E calls its "flagship series" and which elsewhere has been termed "one of cable's true land-

The President's Award nominations include A&E Biography's landmark profiles; above, ER's close look at life and death issues; and If These Walls Could Talk, starring Demi Moore, Cher and Sissy Spacek, below, which explored the abortion issue.

marks" for its in-depth, detailed and historically accurate profiles. The longest-running, single-topic documentary series on television, *Biography* premiered in 1987 as a weekly series, expanding to five nights a week in June 1994, and to six nights in September 1995, with occasional Sunday specials as well. The program now features more than 130 originally produced hours each year, more than any other documentary series on broadcast or cable television, for a series total of nearly 500 profiles. Subjects have ranged from Van Cliburn to the Vanderbilts, Julius Caesar to Sid Caesar, with recently aired profiles featuring Barbara Stanwyck, Roseanne, Arthur Godfrey, Genghis Khan, Malcolm Forbes, Sam Giancana and the Boston Strangler. Winner of the

CableACE for best documentary series, the show has been a finalist for the Golden CableACE, the cable industry's highest honor, and in 1995 received the Creators Award from the National Academy of Cable Programming.

ER on NBC, another repeat nominee and television's highest-rated drama series. The fast-paced, gritty drama, whose large cast is headed by Anthony Edwards and George Clooney, explores the workings of a Chicago teaching hospital and the issues faced by its overburdened emergency room staff. Created by best-selling author Michael Crichton from his own medical experiences, the show has been nominated

continued on page 18

14

Universal Television Group
Proudly Salutes Our
1997 Emmy® Nominees

LAW & ORDER

Outstanding Drama Series

Outstanding Cinematography for a Series
Constantine Makris - "Mad Dog"

Outstanding Single-Camera Picture Editing for a Series
David Siegel - "Judgement In L.A., Part 2"

Outstanding Sound Mixing for a Drama Series
David Platt, William M. Nicholson, Thomas Meloeny - "D-Girl"

SAM WATERSTON

*Outstanding Lead Actor
in a Drama Series*
LAW & ORDER

STOCKARD CHANNING

*Outstanding Lead Actress
in a Miniseries or a Special*
AN UNEXPECTED FAMILY

*Outstanding Music Composition
for a Series (Dramatic Underscore)*
Joseph Loduca - "Destiny"

Outstanding Main Title Theme Music
Mark Isham - "A Terrible Beauty"

Outstanding Main Title Design
Kasumi Mihori, Billy Pittard

UNIVERSAL

Universal Television Group

THE COLUMBIA TRISTAR TELEVISION GROUP THANKS AND CONGRATULATES OUR

Mad About You

Outstanding Comedy Series

Larry Charles, Danny Jacobson, Paul Reiser, Executive Producers

Victor Levin, Richard Day, Co-Executive Producers

Helen Hunt, Bob Heath, Craig Knizek,

Maria Semple, Jenji Kohan, Producers

Mary Connelly, Coordinating Producer

Helen Hunt
Outstanding Actress in a Comedy Series

Paul Reiser
Outstanding Actor in a Comedy Series

Carol Burnett
Outstanding Guest Actress in a Comedy Series

Mel Brooks
Outstanding Guest Actor in a Comedy Series

Sid Caesar
Outstanding Guest Actor in a Comedy Series

The Nanny

Fran Drescher
Outstanding Actress in a Comedy Series

Shawn Holly Cookson, Terry Gordon
Outstanding Individual Achievement in Costuming a Comedy Series

Brenda Cooper
Outstanding Individual Achievement in Costuming a Comedy Series

dark skies

Mike Jones
Outstanding Main Title Design

Michael Hoenig
Outstanding Main Title Theme Music

Early Edition

W.G. Snuffy Walden
Outstanding Main Title Theme Music

W.G. Snuffy Walden
Outstanding Music Composition for a Series (Dramatic Underscore)

Produced By
Brillstein-Grey Entertainment

Luellyn Harper
Outstanding Individual Achievement in Costuming a Comedy Series

LIGHTING UP SCREENS

THE ACADEMY OF TELEVISION ARTS AND SCIENCES
1997 EMMY NOMINEES

THE Larry Sanders SHOW

Produced By
Brillstein-Grey Entertainment

Outstanding Comedy Series

Garry Shandling, Brad Grey, Executive Producers

John Riggi, Jon Vitti, Co-Executive Producers

Becky Hartman Edwards, Carol Leifer, Supervising Producers

John Ziffren, Jeff Cesario, Producers

Todd Holland, Co-Producer

John Markus, Judd Apatow, Earl Pomerantz, Consulting Producers

Garry Shandling
Outstanding Lead Actor in a Comedy Series

Jeffrey Tambor
Outstanding Supporting Actor in a Comedy Series

Rip Torn
Outstanding Supporting Actor in a Comedy Series

Janeane Garafalo
Outstanding Supporting Actress in a Comedy Series

Ellen DeGeneres
Outstanding Guest Actress in a Comedy Series

David Duchovny
Outstanding Guest Actor in a Comedy Series

Alan Myerson
Outstanding Individual Achievement in Directing in a Comedy Series

Todd Holland
Outstanding Individual Achievement in Directing in a Comedy Series

Judd Apatow, John Markus, Teleplay, Garry Shandling, Story
Outstanding Writing for a Comedy Series

Peter Tolan
Outstanding Writing for a Comedy Series

Jon Vitti
Outstanding Writing for a Comedy Series

Leslie Tolan, Paul Anderson
Outstanding Multi-Camera Picture Editing for a Series

Leslie Tolan, Sean Lambert
Outstanding Multi-Camera Picture Editing for a Series

Peter Smokler
Outstanding Lighting Direction (Electronic) for a Series

Ed Moskowitz, Ed Golya, John Bickelhaupt
Outstanding Sound Mixing for a Comedy Series or Special

Seinfeld

Produced By
Castle Rock Entertainment

Outstanding Comedy Series

Jerry Seinfeld, George Shapiro, Howard West, Executive Producers

Peter Mehlman, Co-Executive Producer

Alec Berg, Andy Robin, Jeff Schaffer, Supervising Producers

Andy Ackerman, Suzy Mamann Greenberg,

Tim Kaiser, Gregg Kavet, Producers

Spike Feresten, Dave Mandel, Co-Producers

Tom Gammill, Max Pross, Consulting Producers

Nancy Sprow, Coordinating Producer

Julia Louis-Dreyfus
Outstanding Supporting Actress in a Comedy Series

Jason Alexander
Outstanding Supporting Actor in a Comedy Series

Michael Richards
Outstanding Supporting Actor in a Comedy Series

Jerry Stiller
Outstanding Guest Actor in a Comedy Series

Andy Ackerman
Outstanding Individual Achievement in Directing in a Comedy Series

Peter Mehlman, Jill Franklyn
Outstanding Writing for a Comedy Series

Skip Collector
Outstanding Multi-Camera Picture Editing for a Series

Marc Hirschfeld, Meg Liberman, Bryan Myers
Outstanding Casting for a Series

COLUMBIA TRISTAR

TELEVISION GROUP
a SONY PICTURES ENTERTAINMENT company

WWW.SONY.COM

A R O U N D   T H E   W O R L D

continued from page 14

for more than 60 Emmy Awards in its three seasons, including this year's top number of 22; its eight wins in its first season tied the record for most Emmys won by a series in a single season. It

The other two contenders for the President's Award are, above, Miss Evers' Boys, *which looked at a disturbing episode of our history and, at left,* Touched By An Angel's *groundbreaking spiritual explorations.*

is the recipient of the George Foster Peabody Award.

If These Walls Could Talk on HBO, a film starring Demi Moore, Sissy Spacek and Cher as three women confronting the dilemma of abortion in different social and political climates, from the 1950s to the 1990s. Presented by the HBO NYC movie division, which was launched in 1996 to provide a forum for new and established talent to do contemporary, innovative work, the film looks beyond the politics and legalities to focus on the painful truths women must face when dealing with an unexpected pregnancy. Moore served as an executive producer, while Cher made her directorial debut in the trilogy segment in which she stars.

Miss Evers' Boys on HBO, which depicts a little known chapter in American history in which 600 Southern black men were unknowingly denied treatment for syphilis in a 40-year (1932-

1972) government-funded study to determine the effects of the disease, thereby ascertaining whether blacks were biologically inferior or equal to whites. Based on the Pulitzer Prize-nominated play of the same name, the film stars Alfre Woodard as nurse Evers and Laurence Fishburne as one of the study's subjects, in an examination of racism, medical ethics, social consciousness and personal responsibility. It was produced by HBO NYC in association with Anasazi Productions, which was founded by Ted Danson to produce just such thought-provoking stories. Its total of 12 Emmy nominations is the third-highest number (tying with *The X-Files*) received by a program this year.

Touched by an Angel on CBS, the Sunday night

series which stars Roma Downey, Della Reese and John Dye as a trio of angels sent from heaven to help people at a crossroads in their lives. Interweaving allegories and proverbs with solid story-telling, it imparts spiritual values and the concept of God's love in episodes dealing with everything from homelessness to cancer, rape to juvenile offenders, strained family relations to people with disabilities. In danger of cancellation in its first season, the show, which is entering its fourth season, is now television's second-highest rated drama after *ER* and consistently draws letters from viewers relating its positive, life-changing impact on them.

—L.S.

Take the Emmy Challenge!

Last Sunday, Emmy Awards were bestowed for excellence in the creative arts that are the foundation of television production. Test your ability to pick the winners.

Begin on page 27 and pick the nominees who, in your judgment, deserve an Emmy for each category. Turn to page 22 to check your answers against those who won. The number shown represents the winner's place in the alphabetical sequence of nominees. When your answer matches the judges' selection, check the box. Add up the number of checked boxes and see the scoring shown at the bottom right of page 22 — to see how good a judge you really are.

NYPD BLUE • Steven Bochco Productions

OUTSTANDING DRAMA SERIES

OUTSTANDING LEAD ACTOR IN A DRAMA SERIES

~Dennis Franz as Detective Andy Sipowicz

~Jimmy Smits as Detective Bobby Simone

OUTSTANDING SUPPORTING ACTOR IN A DRAMA SERIES

~Nicholas Turturro as Detective James Martinez

OUTSTANDING SUPPORTING ACTRESS IN A DRAMA SERIES

~Kim Delaney as Detective Diane Russell

OUTSTANDING DIRECTING FOR A DRAMA SERIES

~Mark Tinker • Where's Swaldo?

OUTSTANDING WRITING FOR A DRAMA SERIES

~David Milch, Stephen Gaghan, Michael R. Perry • Where's Swaldo?

~David Mills • Taillight's Last Gleaming

OUTSTANDING ART DIRECTION FOR A SERIES

~Richard C. Hankins, David Smith • A Wrenching Experience

OUTSTANDING CASTING FOR A SERIES

~Junie Lowry Johnson, Alexa L. Fogel

OUTSTANDING SOUND MIXING FOR A DRAMA SERIES

~Joe Kenworthy, Robert Appere, Ken Burton • Unembraceable You

THE 69TH ANNUAL ACADEMY AWARDS • Academy of Motion Picture Arts and Sciences

OUTSTANDING VARIETY, MUSIC OR COMEDY SPECIAL

~Gil Cates, Producer

OUTSTANDING PERFORMANCE IN A VARIETY OR MUSIC PROGRAM

~Billy Crystal

OUTSTANDING DIRECTING FOR A VARIETY OR MUSIC PROGRAM

~Louis J. Horvitz

OUTSTANDING ART DIRECTION FOR A VARIETY OR MUSIC PROGRAM

~Roy Christopher, Elina Katsioula, Michael G. Gallenberg

OUTSTANDING COSTUME DESIGN FOR A VARIETY OR MUSIC PROGRAM

~Ray Aghayan

OUTSTANDING MUSIC DIRECTION

~Bill Conti

OUTSTANDING SOUND MIXING FOR A VARIETY OR MUSIC SERIES OR A SPECIAL

~Edward J. Greene, Tom Vicari, Robert Douglass

ELLEN • Black/Marlens Co. in association with Touchstone Television

OUTSTANDING LEAD ACTRESS IN A COMEDY SERIES

~Ellen DeGeneres as Ellen Morgan

OUTSTANDING GUEST ACTRESS IN A COMEDY SERIES

~Laura Dern as Susan Richmond

OUTSTANDING DIRECTING FOR A COMEDY SERIES

~Gil Junger • The Puppy Episode

OUTSTANDING WRITING FOR A COMEDY SERIES

~Ellen DeGeneres, Mark Driscoll, Dava Savel, Tracy Newman, Jonathan Stark • The Puppy Episode

OUTSTANDING MULTI-CAMERA PICTURE EDITING FOR A SERIES

~Kris Trexler • The Puppy Episode

THE DREW CAREY SHOW • Mohawk Productions Inc., in association with Warner Bros. Television

OUTSTANDING ART DIRECTION FOR A SERIES

John Shaffner, Joe Stewart, Ed McDonald • New York And Queens

OUTSTANDING CHOREOGRAPHY

~Keith Young • Drew's The Other Man

OUTSTANDING COSTUME DESIGN FOR A SERIES

~Julie Rhine • New York And Queens

POLITICALLY INCORRECT WITH BILL MAHER • Brillstein Grey Communications, HBO Downtown Productions

OUTSTANDING VARIETY, MUSIC OR COMEDY SERIES

~Scott Carter, Nancy Geller, Bill Maher, Bernie Brillstein, Brad Grey, Marc Gurvitz, Executive Producers; Douglas M. Wilson, Senior Producer; Kevin E. Hamburger, Supervising Producer

OUTSTANDING PERFORMANCE IN A VARIETY OR MUSIC PROGRAM

~Bill Maher • Episode #4086

OUTSTANDING WRITING FOR A VARIETY OR MUSIC PROGRAM

~Chris Kelly, Frank Ajaye, Scott Carter, Christopher Case Erbland, Al Franken, Jon Hotchkiss, Arianna Huffington, Hayes Jackson, Brian Jacobsmeyer, Bill Kelley, Billy Martin, Bill Maher, Ned Rice, Chris Rock, Geoff Rodkey, Michael Rotman, Jeff Stilson, Eric Weinberg

STEPHEN KING'S THE SHINING • Lakeside Productions, Inc. in association with Warner Bros. Television

OUTSTANDING MINISERIES

OUTSTANDING MAKEUP FOR A MINISERIES OR A SPECIAL

~Bill Corso, Douglas Noe, Tracy Levy, Ve Neill, Barry Koper, Ashlee Peterson, Jill Rockow, Steve Johnsons, Joel Harlow

OUTSTANDING SOUND EDITING FOR A MINISERIES OR A SPECIAL

our 1997 Emmy Nominees.

~Tom deGorter, Peter Bergren, Kenneth Johnson, Brian Thomas Nist, Joseph H. Earle, Jr., Brad Katona, Fric A. Norris, Andrew Ellerd, Linda Keim, Bruce Tanis, Ron Evans, Gary Lewis, Barbara Issak, Paul Longstaffe, James B. Hevenstreit, Stan Jones, Alyson Dee Moore, Ginger Geary • Part 3

HOME IMPROVEMENT • Wind Dancer Production Group in association with Touchstone Television

OUTSTANDING LEAD ACTRESS IN A COMEDY SERIES

~Patricia Richardson as Jill Taylor

OUTSTANDING LIGHTING DIRECTION (ELECTRONIC) FOR A COMEDY SERIES

~Donald A. Morgan • I Was A Teenage Taylor

OUTSTANDING SOUND MIXING FOR A COMEDY SERIES OR A SPECIAL

~Klaus Landsberg, Charlie McDaniel, Kathy Oldham, John Bickelhaupt • Wilson's World

GUN • Sadwith Productions and Sandcastle V in association with Kushner-Locke

OUTSTANDING CINEMATOGRAPHY FOR A SERIES

~Roy Wagner • Ricochet

OUTSTANDING MAIN TITLE DESIGN

~Jennifer Grey, Earl Jenshus, Billy Pittard

MUPPETS TONIGHT• Jim Henson Productions, Inc.

OUTSTANDING ART DIRECTION FOR A VARIETY OR MUSIC PROGRAM

~Val Strazovec, Jim Dultz, Jenny Wilkinson • Host: Jason Alexander

OUTSTANDING TECHNICAL DIRECTION/ CAMERA/VIDEO FOR A SERIES

~Kenneth Tamburri, Diane Biederbeck, Thomas Conkright, Tom Green, Randy Gomez, Ray Gonzales, Brian Reason, John Palacio,Jr. •Host: Sandra Bullock

ABOUT US: The Dignity Of Children • Fred Berner Films and The Children's Dignity Project in association with Worth Associates, Inc.

OUTSTANDING CHILDREN'S PROGRAM

~Fred Berner, Debra Reynolds, Jeffrey D. Jacobs, Executive Producers; Tracey A. Mitchell, Supervising Producer; Lesley Karsten, Producer; Elaine Frontain Bryant, Associate Producer

FIRST DO NO HARM • Jaffe/Braunstein Films, Ltd.

OUTSTANDING LEAD ACTRESS IN A MINISERIES OR A SPECIAL

~Meryl Streep as Lori Reimuller

HAPPY BIRTHDAY ELIZABETH: A Celebration Of Life • Gary L. Pudney in association with Tall Pony Productions for Greengrass Productions

OUTSTANDING MULTI-CAMERA PICTURE EDITING FOR A MINISERIES OR A SPECIAL

~Michael Polito

SPIN CITY • UBU Productions and Lottery Hill Entertainment in association with DreamWorks Television

OUTSTANDING LEAD ACTOR IN A COMEDY SERIES

~Michael J. Fox as Michael Flaherty

MURDER ONE • Steven Bochco Productions

OUTSTANDING GUEST ACTOR IN A DRAMA SERIES

~Pruitt Taylor Vince as Clifford Banks

RELATIVITY • The Bedford Falls Co., in association with Twentieth Century Fox Television

OUTSTANDING CINEMATOGRAPHY FOR A SERIES

~Michael D. O'Shea • Karen And Her Sisters

SABRINA, THE TEENAGE WITCH • Hartbreak Films & Finishing The Hat in association with Viacom Productions

OUTSTANDING COSTUME DESIGN FOR A SERIES

~Dianne Kennedy • Third Aunt From The Sun

TO LOVE, HONOR, AND DECEIVE • Robert Greenwald Productions / ABC Productions

OUTSTANDING CINEMATOGRAPHY FOR A MINI-SERIES OR A SPECIAL

~Michael D. O'Shea

And the Emmy Went To . . .

See page 19 for instructions. The number shown after each category indicates the winner among the alphabetical sequence of nominees on the page shown.

Scoring	
Boxes checked	
0 - 9	Hope you're enjoying your visit to the entertainment capital of the world.
10 - 24	Pretty good! You do know what it takes to create good television!
25 +	Obviously, you're a long-time industry insider!

Why is Broadway closed on Sunday nights?

We like to think *Mobil Masterpiece Theatre* has something to do with it. That Broadway shuts down, if not to honor television's longest running quality series, at least to enjoy it. For 26 years, *Mobil Masterpiece Theatre* has been a stand-out achievement in American television, and we have been its only sponsor. It has won 27 Emmys so far, and this year the program *Prime Suspect V* and actresses Helen Mirren (*Prime Suspect V*) and Diana Rigg (*Rebecca*) have been nominated. We offer our congratulations to the nominees, and our thanks to PBS, to WGBH in Boston, to the Academy of Television Arts & Sciences and to our loyal audience. It's an honor, as always, to have played a supporting role. For more about Mobil, our newest show is always on. At www.mobil.com.

Mobil The energy to make a difference.™

This year three unrelated recipients have been named to share the Governors Award, a first since the prestigious honor's 1978 inception. The award is voted by the Board of Governors of the Academy, which in 1995 changed its scope to de-emphasize an individual's career accomplishments in favor of a company or organization's current achievements.

And the winners are:

"ABC's March Against Drugs," an unprecedented public service campaign which ran during the month of March 1997. It was designed to encourage parents and children to talk about the dangers of drug abuse, based on findings that children who learn about the risks of drugs from their parents are half as likely to use them. More than 50 different public service announcements featuring ABC news, sports and entertainment personalities were run a total of 437 times, reaching an estimated 142 million viewers. In addition, the network's news, daytime, entertainment and sports divisions aired relevant programming, including special programs on the dangers of substance abuse. Parents' and educators' guides were produced and distributed, and special online sites for parents and children created. The campaign concluded with the broadcast of an *ABC News Town Hall Meeting* during which parents, teachers, children and experts discussed the issues of drug addiction and its consequences.

The second recipient is HBO's *Comic Relief*, whose seven specials have raised more than $40 million for Health Care for the Homeless projects in 23 American cities, and which last fall celebrated its 10th anniversary. Hosted by Billy Crystal, Whoopi Goldberg and Robin Williams, the specials have featured such diverse comedy stars as Roseanne, Dennis Miller, Paula Poundstone, Sinbad, Howie Mandel, Jerry Lewis, Don Rickles and Jon Lovitz.

One hundred percent of the money raised is allocated to health care and related services, so far assisting more than one million homeless Americans. Comic Relief's operators (800-528-1000) remain open 24 hours a day for pledges and donations.

The third recipient is Jac Venza, executive producer of *Great Performances* on PBS, which celebrates its 25th anniversary this November and has become the longest-running performing arts series in the history of television. A former CBS designer, director and producer, Venza conceived and launched the series, which is produced by Thirteen/WNET in New York and has won 50

The three recipients of the Governors Awards: at left, Great Performances *Executive Producer Jac Venza; (top) ABC's March Against Drugs; and* Comic Relief. *Hosts Billy Crystal, Whoopi Goldberg and Robin Williams are shown above.*

Emmy Awards. In doing so, he created a long-before-cable home for everything from spirituals to symphonies, theater to tap dancing, Broadway to grand opera, in some cases spotlighting previously little known talents such as Luciano Pavarotti, Meryl Streep, Swoosie Kurtz, Glenn Close and playwright Wendy Wasserstein.

The Television Academy salutes these exceptional endeavors.

GOVERNORS AWARD RECIPIENTS		
1978 William S. Paley	1986 Red Skelton	1993 and 1994 No awards given
1979 Walter Cronkite	1987 Grant Tinker	1995 PBS
1980 Johnny Carson	1988 William Hanna and Joseph	1996 USA Network's "Erase the
1981 Elton H. Rule	Barbera	Hate" Campaign and
1982 Hallmark Cards, Inc. for	1989 Lucille Ball	TNT's Native American
the *Hallmark Hall of Fame*	1990 Leonard H. Goldenson	Initiative
1983 Sylvester (Pat) Weaver	1991 Mobil Masterpiece Theatre	1997 "ABC's March Against
1984 Bob Hope	(its 20th anniversary season)	Drugs," HBO's *Comic Relief*,
1985 Alistair Cooke	1992 R.E. (Ted) Turner	and Jac Venza.

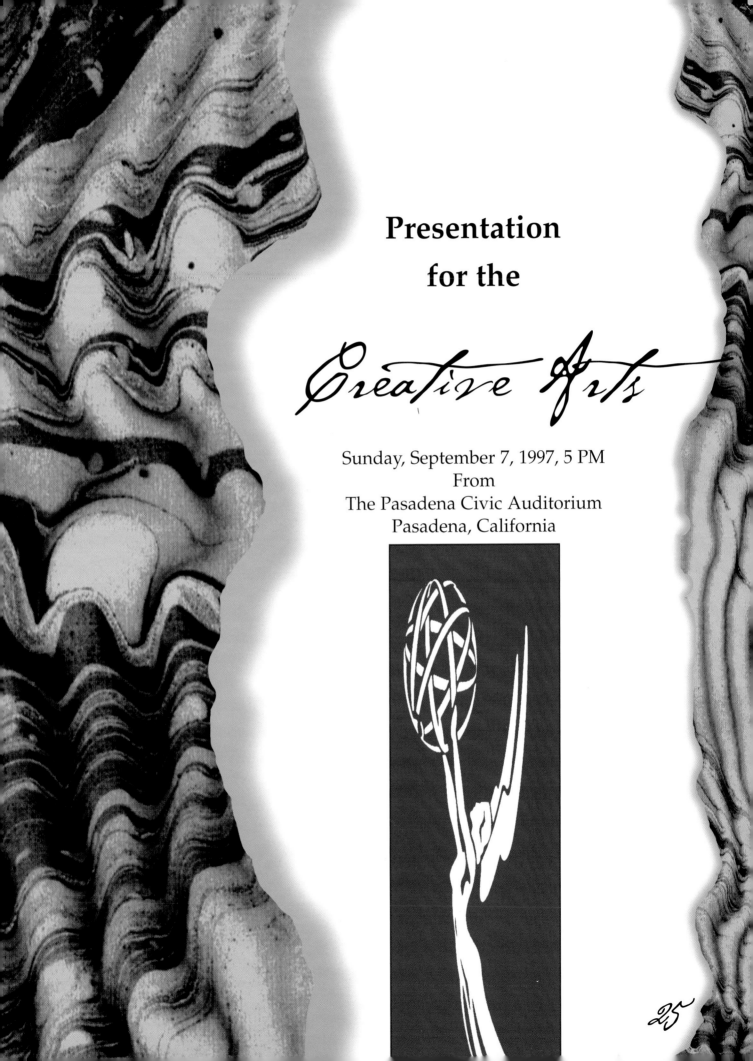

Presentation
for the

Creative Arts

Sunday, September 7, 1997, 5 PM
From
The Pasadena Civic Auditorium
Pasadena, California

25

THE 1997 ANNUAL EMMY AWARDS
PRESENTATION FOR THE CREATIVE ARTS

Show Committee Chair
BILL ALLEN

Producer/Director
SPIKE JONES, JR.

Co-Producers	*Talent Executive*	*Banquet Producer*
JOHN LEVERENCE	BARBARA CHASE	CARLEEN CAPPELLETTI
JULIE CARROLL SHORE		

Talent Coordinators
GINA JONES
TRACY MEDEIROS
JEROMY OLSON
EDYE SCHNEIDER

Consultant Extraordinare
DEE BAKER

Script Supervisor
ANNEMARIE CRIVELLI

Main Title Design & Show Graphics
NANCY TOKOS AND ASSOCIATES

Associate Director	*Technical Director*
PAUL FORREST	ERIC BECKER

Camera Operators	*Stage Managers*
KERRY ASMUSSEN	FRANK AGNONE
JOE BARNES	JOHN ESPOSITO
CRAIG HAMPTON	COURTNEY PHILBROOK
WAYNE KELLY	

Unit Manager	*Seating Coordinator*
SCOTT PALAAZO	LOUISE DANTON

Audio	*Video Control*	*Tape Operator*	*Engineer in Charge*
EVAN ADELMAN	KEITH ANDERSON	STEVE ELLIS	DOUG ARMSTRONG

Mobile Production Facilities Provided By Camera Ready Productions
Production Support Provided by Goldberg and O'Reily Entertainment
Design and Coordination Provided by Merv Griffen Productions
The Academy wishes to express its appreciation to the presenters and to the many shows that
provided special video material.

Announcers
EARL BOEN & LOU HUNT

FOR THE ACADEMY

President
RICHARD H. FRANK

Executive Director
JAMES. L. LOPER

Chief Financial And Administrative Officer
HERB JELLINEK

National Awards Chair
GEORGE A. SUNGA

Governors Award Chair
MERYL C. MARSHALL

Awards Director
JOHN LEVERENCE

Primetime Awards Administrator
JULIE CARROLL SHORE

Public Relations Director
MURRAY WEISSMAN

ART DIRECTION FOR A SERIES

John Shaffner, Production Designer; Joe Stewart, Art Director;
Ed McDonald, Set Decorator
The Drew Carey Show • New York And Queens • ABC • Mohawk Productions Inc., in association with Warner Bros. Television

Richard C. Hunkins, Production Designer; David Smith, Set Decorator
NYPD Blue • A Wrenching Experience • ABC • Steven Bochco Productions

Patricia van Ryker, Production Designer; Mary Ann Good, Set Decorator
7th Heaven • The Color Of God • WB • Spelling Television, Inc.

Herman Zimmerman, Production Designer; Randall McIlvain, Art Director; Laura Richarz, Set Decorator
Star Trek: Deep Space Nine • Trials And Tribble-ations • Syndicated • Star Trek: Deep Space Nine Production in association with Paramount Pictures

Graeme Murray, Production Designer; Gary P. Allen, Art Director; Shirley Inget, Set Decorator
The X-Files • Memento Mori • FOX • Ten Thirteen Productions in association with 20th Century Fox Television

ART DIRECTION FOR A MINISERIES OR A SPECIAL

Trevor Williams, Production Designer; Jozsef Romvari, Art Director; Andras Maros, Set Decorator
The Hunchback • TNT • Alliance Communications & TNT in association with Adelson/Baumgarten

Don Taylor, Production Designer; Jo Graysmark, Art Direction; John Bush, Set Decorator
Jane Austen's Emma • A&E • United Film & Television Productions for Meridian Broadcasting in association with Chestermead Ltd. and Chestermead Ltd. and A&E Network

Hub Braden, Production Designer; Mary Dodson, Art Director; Ellen Totleben, Set Decorator
Mrs. Santa Claus • CBS • Hallmark Entertainment in association with Corymore Productions

Roger Hall, Production Designer; John King, Supervising Art Director; Frederic Evard, Art Director (Turkey); Karen Brookes, Set Decorator
The Odyssey • Part II • NBC • Hallmark Entertainment in association with American Zoetrope

Charles Rosen, Production Designer; Charles Butcher, Charles Breen, Art Directors; Stephanie Ziemer, Linda Spheeris, Set Decorators
Weapons Of Mass Distraction • HBO • Massive Productions, Inc. in association with HBO Pictures

ART DIRECTION FOR A VARIETY OR MUSIC PROGRAM

Roy Christopher, Production Designer; Elina Katsioula, Michael G. Gallenberg, Art Directors
The 69th Annual Academy Awards • ABC • Academy of Motion Picture Arts and Sciences

Bob DeMora, Production Designer
Bette Midler: Diva Las Vegas • HBO • A Miss M Production in association with Cream Cheese Films and HBO Original Programming

Bob Keene, Production Designer; Steve Bass, Art Director
Centennial Olympic Games: Opening Ceremonies • NBC • Don Mischer Productions

Val Strazovec, Production Designer; Jim Dultz, Art Director; Jenny Wilkinson, Set Decorator
Muppets Tonight • Host: Jason Alexander • ABC • Jim Henson Productions, Inc.

Toby Corbett, Production Designer; Chez Cherry, Art Director; Kristen Messina, Set Decorator
Tracey Takes On... • Vegas • HBO • Takes On Productions, Inc.

Emmy Nomination Announcement Garners Two Firsts

There were two firsts regarding the announcement of the nominations for tonight's 49th annual Primetime Emmy Awards, held at 5:35 A.M. Pacific time July 24 at the Television Academy's Leonard H. Goldenson Theatre and hosted by ATAS president Richard H. Frank and two-time Emmy Award winner Dana Delany.

One first was the attendance by American Chinese Television, which broadcasts in Chinese with English subtitles. The company's representatives were among the 250 press members, publicists and photographers who turned out for the event. Other media included all the morning television shows, United States wire services and the international wire service Reuters; there was live coverage on the radio and the Internet.

The other first was the live hour-long coverage by E! Entertainment. Not only did the cable network air the announcement, but three critics then discussed and analyzed the nominations and interviewed Frank, Delany and Emmy Award ceremony executive producer Don Mischer.   — L.S.

CONGRATULATIONS

TO ALL THE EMMY NOMINEES ON YOUR FINE ACHIEVEMENTS

SERIES

JAMES BAGDONAS, A.S.C. ....Chicago Hope—*A Time to Kill*

ROY WAGNER, A.S.C. ....Gun—*Ricochet*

CONSTANTINE MAKRIS ....Law & Order—*Mad Dog*

MICHAEL D. O'SHEA, A.S.C. ....Relativity—*Karen and Her Sisters*

JONATHAN WEST, A.S.C. ....Star Trek: Deep Space Nine—*Apocalypse Rising*

MINISERIES or SPECIAL

ALAR KIVILO...*Gotti*

JAMES BAGDONAS, A.S.C. ....*Hidden In America*

FRED ELMES, A.S.C. ....*In The Gloaming*

DONALD M. MORGAN, A.S.C. ....*Miss Ever's Boys*

MICHAEL D. O'SHEA, A.S.C. ....*To Love, Honor and Deceive*

GUEST ACTOR IN A DRAMA SERIES

Alan Arkin as Zoltan Karpathein
Chicago Hope • CBS • David E. Kelley Productions in association with 20th Century Fox

Louis Gossett, Jr. as Anderson Walker
Touched By An Angel • CBS • CBS Productions in association with Moon Water Productions

William H. Macy as Dr. Morgenstern
ER • NBC • Constant c Productions, Amblin Television in association with Warner Bros. Television

Ewan McGregor as Duncan Stewart
ER • NBC • Constant c Productions, Amblin Television in association with Warner Bros. Television

Pruitt Taylor Vince as Clifford Banks
Murder One • ABC • Steven Bochco Productions

CONGRATULATIONS

TO ALL THE EMMY NOMINEES ON YOUR FINE ACHIEVEMENTS

OUTSTANDING COMMERCIAL

GM EV-1 ....*Appliances*
Industrial Light & Magic - Production Company
Hal Riney & Partners - Ad Agency

HBO ....*Chimps*
PYTKA - Production Company
BBDO - Ad Agency

LEVI'S ....*Doctor*
Satellite - Production Company
Foote, Cone & Belding - Ad Agency

LEVI'S ....*Elevator Fantasy*
Propaganda Films - Production Company
Foote, Cone & Belding - Ad Agency

NIKE..*Hello World*
PYTKA - Production Company
Wieden & Kennedy - Ad Agency

ACHIEVEMENT IN CULTURAL PROGRAMMING — PERFORMANCE

(AREA AWARD: POSSIBILITY OF ONE OR MORE THAN ONE AWARD GIVEN)

Pilobolus Dance Theatre Performers
John F. Kennedy Center 25th Anniversary Celebration • PBS • A production of the John F. Kennedy Center for the Performing Arts in association with Smith-Hemion and WETA, Washington, D.C.

Dance Theatre Of Harlem Performers
John F. Kennedy Center 25th Anniversary Celebration • PBS • A production of the John F. Kennedy Center for the Performing Arts in association with Smith-Hemion and WETA, Washington, D.C.

CULTURAL MUSIC-DANCE PROGRAM

Bobby McFerrin: Loosely Mozart, The New Innovators Of Classical Music - Great Performances • PBS • Sony Classical in association with Thriteen/WNET
Peter Gelb, Executive Producer; Pat Jaffe, Executive Producer/ Director; Molly McBride, Laura Mitgang, Producers; Bobby McFerrin, Host/Performer

A Celebration Of The American Musical - Live From Lincoln Center • PBS • Lincoln Center for The Performing Arts, Inc.
John Goberman, Producer; Marc Bauman, Coordinating Producer

John F. Kennedy Center 25th Anniversary Celebration • PBS • A production of the John F. Kennedy Center for the Performing Arts in association with Smith-Hemion and WETA, Washington, D.C.
Lawrence J. Wilker, Executive Producer; Gary Smith, Executive Producer/Producer/Writer; Fred A. Rappoport, Producer/Writer; Robert Shrum, Writer; Dwight Hemion, Director

Mostly Mozart 30th Anniversary Opening Night Concert With Itzhak Perlman and Pinchas Zukerman - Live From Lincoln Center • PBS • Lincoln Center for The Performing Arts, Inc.
John Goberman, Producer; Marc Bauman, Coordinating Producer

Puccini's "La Boheme" With The New York City Opera - Live From Lincoln Center • PBS • Lincoln Center for The Performing Arts, Inc.
John Goberman, Producer; Marc Bauman, Coordinating Producer

CASTING FOR A SERIES

John Levey, C.S.A., Casting Executive; Barbara Miller, C.S.A., Executive In Charge Of Casting
ER • NBC • Constant c̲ Productions, Amblin Television in association with Warner Bros. Television

Jeff Greenberg, C.S.A., Casting Executive
Frasier • NBC • Grub Street Productions in association with Paramount

Lou Digiamo, Pat Moran, C.S.A., Brett Goldstein, Casting Executives
Homicide: Life On The Street • NBC • NBC Productions in association with Baltimore Pictures and Fatima Productions

Junie Lowry Johnson, Casting Executive; Alexa L. Fogel, New York Casting Executive
NYPD Blue • ABC • Steven Bochco Productions

Marc Hirschfeld, Meg Liberman, Brian Myers, Casting Executives
Seinfeld • NBC • Castle Rock Entertainment

CASTING FOR A MINISERIES OR A SPECIAL

Linda Lowy, Casting Executive
Bastard Out Of Carolina • Showtime • Gary Hoffman Productions, Inc.

Lynn Stalmaster, Casting Executive
Crime Of The Century • HBO • Astoria Productions in association with HBO Pictures

April Webster, C.S.A., Casting Executive
Grand Avenue • HBO • Wildwood Enterprises and Elsboy Entertainment

Jaki Brown-Karman, Robyn M. Mitchell, Shay Bentley-Griffin, C.S.A., Casting Executives
Miss Evers' Boys • HBO • An Anasazi Production in association with
HBO NYC

Gary M. Zuckerbrod, C.S.A., Casting Executive
Weapons Of Mass Distraction • HBO • Massive Productions, Inc. in association with HBO Pictures

CHOREOGRAPHY
(AREA AWARD: POSSIBILITY OF ONE OR MORE THAN ONE AWARD GIVEN)

Keith Young, Choreographer
The Drew Carey Show • Drew's The Other Man • ABC • Mohawk Productions Inc., in association with Warner Bros. Television

Dianne McIntyre, Choreographer
Miss Evers' Boys • HBO • An Anasazi Production in association with HBO NYC

Rob Marshall, Choreographer
Mrs. Santa Claus • CBS • Hallmark Entertainment in association with Corymore Productions

Sarah Kawahara, Choreographer
Scott Hamilton: Upside Down • CBS • Insight Production Co., Ltd. in association with Buena Vista Television

Marguerite Derricks, Choreography
3rd Rock From The Sun • A Nightmare On Dick Street • NBC • Carsey-Werner Productions, LLC

Paul Taylor, Choreography
The Wrecker's Ball: Three Dances By Paul Taylor • PBS • A Thirteen/WNET Production in association with RM Associates

SOUND EDITING FOR A SERIES

Richard Taylor, Supervising Sound Editor; Kenneth Johnson, Linda L. Keim, Brian Thomas Nist, Peter Bergren, Sound Effects Editors; Barbara Issak, Dialogue Editor; Eric Mellor Erickson, James B. Hebenstreit, ADR Editors
The Cape • Pilot • Syndicated • MTM Enterprises, Inc. in association with ZM Productions

David Weathers, Supervising Sound Editor; Doug Kent, Supervising Sound Effects Editor; Bob Moore, Mark Cookson, Sound Effects Editor; David Grecu, David Beadle, Tom Scurry, Dan Tripoli, Dialogue Editors; Jane Boegel, ADR Editor; Kim Naves, Music Editor
Chicago Hope • Day Of The Rope • CBS • David E. Kelley Productions in association with 20th Century Fox

Albert J. Ibbotson, Supervising Sound Editor; Steffan Falesitch, Dialogue Editor; David M. Cowan, Dialogue/ADR Editor; Charlie Shepard, Jonathan Golodner, Carmine Rubino, Sound Effects Editors; Timothy A. Pearson, Matt Dettmann, Foley Artists; Dino Moriana, Music Editor
Nash Bridges • Zodiac • CBS • Don Johnson Company & Carlton Cuse Productions in association with Rysher Entertainment

Peter Austin, Supervising Sound Editor; Michael Thomas Babcock, Linda L. Keim, Kenneth Johnson, Sound Effects Editors; Paul Longstaffe, Warren Smith, Dialogue Editors; Kim Naves, Music Editor
Profiler • Cruel and Unusual • NBC • NBC Studios

Thierry J. Couturier, Supervising Sound Editor; Stuart Calderon, Ira Leslie, Maciek Malish, Debra Ruby-Winsberg, Chris Fradkin, Jay Levine, Chris Reeves, Susan Welsh, Sound Editors; Jeff Charbonneau, Music Editor; Gary Marullo, Foley Artist; Mike Salvetta, Foley Artist
The X-Files • Tempus Fugit • FOX • Ten Thirteen Productions in association with 20th Century Fox Television

SOUND EDITING FOR A MINISERIES OR A SPECIAL

David Hankins, Supervising Sound Editor; Eric A. Norris, Myron Nettinga, Bruce Tanis, Sound Effects Editors; Laura Laird, Sound Editor; Dennis Gray, Ron Evans, Ralph Osborn, Dialogue Editors; Dean Richard Marino, Music Editor; Alyson Dee Moore, Nancy May Parker, Foley Artists
The Cherokee Kid • HBO • Spring Creek Productions in association with Afros and Bellbottoms Productions

Rich Harrison, Supervising Sound Editor; Tom Cornwell, Charles Dayton, Peter Harrison, Rick Hinson, Sound Editors; Tally Paulos, James N. Harrison, ADR Editors; Virginia Sue Ellsworth, Music Editor; Gregg Barbanell, Michael Broomberg, Foley Artists
Crazy Horse • TNT • Von Zerneck/Sertner Films

Bill Bell, Supervising Editor; Kristi Johns, ADR Editor; Anton Holden, Adriane Marfiak, Mike Lyle, Bob Costanza, Mark Steele, Rob Webber, Gary Macheel, M.P.S.E., Rusty Tinsley, Lou Thomas, Tim Terusa, David Eichhorn, M.P.S.E., Rick Steele, John Levy, Sound Editors; Sharon Smith, Music Editor; Tim Chilton, Jill Schachne, Foley Artists
David • Part 1 • TNT • TNT, LUX, BetaTaurus and RAI

Tom deGorter, Supervising Sound Editor; Peter Bergren, Kenneth Johnson, Brian Thomas Nist, Joseph H. Earle, Jr., Brad Katona, Eric A. Norris, Andrew Ellerd, Linda L. Keim, Bruce Tanis, Sound Effects Editors; Ron Evans, Gary Lewis, Barbara Issak, Paul Longstaffe, Dialogue Editors; James B. Hebenstreit, ADR Editor; Stan Jones, Music Editor; Alyson Dee Moore, Ginger Geary, Foley Artists
Stephen King's The Shining • Part 3 • ABC • Lakeside Productions, Inc. in association with Warner Bros. Television

Stephen Grubbs, Supervising Sound Editor; David Scharf, Charles V. Bruce, Lloyd J. Keiser, Kevin Fisher, Philip Jamtaas, Sound Editors; Marty Wereski, Music Editor; Adam J. DeCoster, Paige N. Pollack, Foley Artists
William Faulkner's Old Man (Hallmark Hall of Fame Presentation) • CBS • Hallmark Hall Fame Productions, Inc.

AWARD

ABC's March Against Drugs campaign that presented more than 400 network PSA's and special programs during March, 1997 on the dangers of substance abuse.

Comic Relief, HBO's seven Robin Williams-Billy Crystal-Whoopi Goldberg hosted benefit specials that have disbursed more than $35 million to homeless American projects over the past 10 years.

Jac Venza, executive producer of PBS's "Great Performances" programs of ballets, concerts and special performances that are about to enter their 25th year.

NATPE®

CONGRATULATES

ALL THE

NOMINEES

AND WINNERS

OF THE

1997 EMMY AWARDS

NATPE is the world's leading
nonprofit television programming and
software association dedicated to the
continued growth and success of the
global television marketplace.

Visit our Web site at **www.natpe.org**

2425 OLYMPIC BOULEVARD, SUITE 550E
SANTA MONICA, CALIFORNIA 90404
TEL: 310-453-4440 · FAX: 310-453-5258

COSTUMING FOR A SERIES

Paul Dafelmair, Costume Supervisor
JAG   • Cowboys & Cossacks   • CBS • Belisarius Productions in association with Paramount Network Television

Shawn-Holly Cookson, Terry Gordon, Costumers
The Nanny   • The Facts Of Lice   • CBS • Sternin/Fraser Ink, Inc. and High School Sweethearts in association with TriStar Television

Brenda Cooper, Costumer
The Nanny   • The Rosie Show   • CBS • Sternin/Fraser Ink, Inc. and High School Sweethearts in association with TriStar Television

Luellyn Harper, Costume Supervisor
NewsRadio   • Awards Show   • NBC • BGC Productions, Inc.

COSTUMING FOR A MINISERIES OR A SPECIAL

(AREA AWARD: POSSIBILITY OF ONE OR NO AWARD GIVEN)

Andy Gordon, Head Costumer
Disney's "The Hunchback Of Notre Dame" Festival Of Fun Musical Spectacular   • Disney Channel • Brad Lachman Productions in association with The Disney Channel

GUEST ACTRESS IN A DRAMA SERIES

Veronica Cartwright as Norma
ER • NBC • Constant c Productions, Amblin Television in association with Warner Bros. Television

Diane Ladd as Carolyn Sellers
Touched By An Angel • CBS • CBS Productions in association with Moon Water Productions

Anne Meara as Donna DiGrazi
Homicide: Life On The Street • NBC • NBC Productions in association with Baltimore Pictures and Fatima Productions

Isabella Rossellini as Prof. Marina Gianni
Chicago Hope • CBS • David E. Kelley Productions in association with 20th Century Fox

Dianne Wiest as Lillian Hepworth
Avonlea • Disney Channel • Sullivan Entertainment Inc. with C.B.C., The Disney Channel, Telefilm Canada

HAIRSTYLING FOR A SERIES

Karl Wesson, Key Hairstylist; Kelly Kline, Hairstylist to Jane Seymour; Deborah Dobson, Virginia Grobeson, Christine Lee, Leslie Anne Anderson, Hairstylists
Dr. Quinn, Medicine Woman • Starting Over • CBS • CBS Entertainment Productions/The Sullivan Company

Norma Lee, Key Hairstylist; Brian Andrew-Tunstall, Jacklin Masteran, Linle White, Francine Shermaine, Caryl Codon, Susan Zettlow Maust, Charlotte Harvey, Hairstylists
Star Trek: Deep Space Nine • Trials And Tribble-ations • Syndicated • Star Trek: Deep Space Nine Production in association with Paramount Pictures

Josée Normand, Key Hairstylist; Suzan Bagdadi, Karen Asano Myers, Monique De Sart, Charlotte Gravenor, Jo Ann Phillips, Frank Fontaine, Diane Pepper, Hairstylists
Star Trek: Voyager • Fair Trade • UPN • Star Trek: Voyager production in association with Paramount Pictures

Pixie Schwartz, Camille Friend, Hairstylists
3rd Rock From The Sun • A Nightmare On Dick Street • NBC • Carsey-Werner Productions, LLC

Audree Futterman, Key Hairstylist
Tracey Takes On... • Childhood • HBO • Takes On Productions, Inc.

HAIRSTYLING FOR A MINISERIES OR A SPECIAL

Roberto Ramos, Hairstylist
Bette Midler: Diva Las Vegas • HBO • A Miss M Production in association with Cream Cheese Films and HBO Original Programming

Joani Yarbrough, Jojo Guthrie, Jeaneen Muckerman, Hairstylists
Crazy Horse • TNT • Von Zerneck/Sertner Films

Bogyo Kajtar, Key Hairstylist; Libus Bernova, Hairdresser
The Hunchback • TNT • Alliance Communications & TNT in association with Adelson/Baumgarten

Clare Corsick, Key Hairstylist; Enzo Angileri, Hairstylist to Ms. Moore; Sally Harper, Hairstylist to Ms. Spacek; Voni Hinkle, Serena Radaelli, Renata Leuschner, Hairstylists to Cher; Cammy Langer, Hairstylist
If These Walls Could Talk • HBO • A Moving Pictures Production

Gloria Montemayor, Key Hairstylist; Lola "Skip" McNalley, Dorothy Andre, Hairstylists
Mrs. Santa Claus • CBS • Hallmark Entertainment in association with Corymore Productions

Suzanne Stokes-Munton, Chief Hairdresser; Petra Schaumann, Hairdresser
The Odyssey • NBC • Hallmark Entertainment in association with American Zoetrope

Congratulations

MUSIC COMPOSITION FOR A SERIES (DRAMATIC UNDERSCORE)

Louis Febre, John Debney, Composers
The Cape • Pilot • Syndicated • MTM Enterprises, Inc. in association with ZM Productions

W.G. Snuffy Walden, Composer
Early Edition • The Choice • CBS •Three Characters Inc./Angelica Films/CBS Productions in association with TriStar Television

David Langley Hamilton, Composer
Orleans • Pilot • CBS • Samoset Inc. in association with Paramount Pictures Studio

Mark Snow, Composer
The X-Files • Paper Hearts • FOX • Ten Thirteen Productions in association with 20th Century Fox Television

Joseph LoDuca, Composer
Xena: Warrior Princess • Destiny • Syndicated • Renaissance Pictures in association with Universal Television

MUSIC COMPOSITION FOR A MINISERIES OR A SPECIAL (DRAMATIC UNDERSCORE)

Patrick Williams, Composer
After Jimmy • CBS • Holiday Productions in association with Spelling Television, Inc.

Ernest Troost, Composer
Calm At Sunset • CBS • Hallmark Hall of Fame Productions, Inc.

Mark Mothersbaugh, Composer
Quicksilver Highway • FOX • National Studios

Bruce Broughton, Composer
True Women • CBS • Craig Anderson Productions in association with Hallmark Entertainment

Laurence Rosenthal, Composer
The Young Indiana Jones Chronicles: Travels With Father • Family Channel • Lucasfilm, Ltd., in association With Amblin Entertainment and The Family Channel

Congratulations To Remember WENN, The Critically Acclaimed Series Entering Its 3rd Year, For Its Emmy® Nomination

Outstanding Costume Design For A Series
Carolyn Grifel - Costume Designer, Remember WENN

AMERICAN MOVIE CLASSICS

MUSIC DIRECTION

Bill Conti, Music Director
The 69th Annual Academy Awards   • ABC • Academy of Motion Picture Arts and Sciences

Bobby Lyle, Music Director
Bette Midler: Diva Las Vegas   • HBO • A Miss M Production in association with Cream Cheese Films and HBO Original Programming

Mark Watters, Music Director
Centennial Olympic Games: Opening Ceremonies   • NBC • Don Mischer Productions

Ian Fraser, Music Director
The 53rd Presidential Inaugural Gala   • CBS • Smith-Hemion Productions

Alf Clausen, Music Director
The Simpsons   • Simpsoncalifragilisticexpiali (Annoyed Grunt) cious   • FOX • Gracie Films in association with Twentieth Television

MUSIC AND LYRICS

Michael Silversher, Patty Silversher, Music & Lyrics
Boo! To You Too, Winnie The Pooh   • CBS • Song Title: "I Wanna Scare Myself"   • Walt Disney Television Animation

David Foster, Kenneth "Babyface" Edmonds, Composers; Linda Thompson, Lyricist
Centennial Olympic Games: Opening Ceremonies   • NBC • Song Title: "The Power Of The Dream"   • Don Mischer Productions

Mark Watters, Composer; Lorraine Feather, Lyricist
Centennial Olympic Games: Opening Ceremonies   • NBC • Song Title: "Faster, Higher, Stronger"   • Don Mischer Productions

Jerry Herman, Composer/Lyricist
Mrs. Santa Claus   • CBS • Song Title: "Mrs. Santa Claus"   • Hallmark Entertainment in association with Corymore Productions

Alf Clausen, Music; Ken Keeler, Lyrics
The Simpsons   • Bart After Dark   • FOX • Song Title: "We Put The Spring In Springfield"   • Gracie Films in association with Twentieth Television

MAIN TITLE THEME MUSIC

John Debney, Composer
The Cape • Syndicated • MTM Enterprises, Inc. in association with ZM Productions

Danny Lux, Composer
Crisis Center • NBC • A Thania St. John Project, Viacom Productions in association with NBC Studios

Michael Hoenig, Composer
Dark Skies • NBC • Bryce Zabel Productions in association with Columbia Pictures Television

W.G. Snuffy Walden, Composer
Early Edition • CBS • Three Characters Inc./Angelica Films/ CBS Productions in association with TriStar Television

Mark Isham, Composer
EZ Streets • CBS • Paul Haggis Productions in association with Universal Television

The Emmys in Europe

Arlington Productions Executive Producer Kevin Francis (second from left), is seen presenting several 1996 Emmys to his countrymen in his capacity as honorary representative of the Television Academy in the United Kingdom and Europe. John Fenner (far left) and Alan Tomkins (far right) won for outstanding achievement in art direction for a miniseries or special for their work on NBC's *Gulliver's Travels*. Richard Ganniclift (second from right) won his Emmy for outstanding achievement in informational programming for his work on TBS' *The Private Life of Plants*.

outsta

buffy the vampire slayer

Makeup for a Series
Todd A. McIntosh, John Maldonado,
John Wheaton, John Vulich

chicago hope

Drama Series
David E. Kelley Productions, Inc.
in association with
Twentieth Century Fox Television

Lead Actress in a Drama Series
Christine Lahti

Supporting Actor in a Drama Series
Adam Arkin

Supporting Actor in a Drama Series
Hector Elizondo

Guest Actor in a Drama Series
Alan Arkin

Guest Actress in a Drama Series
Isabella Rossellini

Cinematography for a Series
James R. Bagdonas, A.S.C.

Single-Camera Picture Editing for a Series
Alec Smight, A.C.E., Mark Baldwin,
Augie Hess

Sound Editing for a Series
Dave Weathers, Doug Kent, Robert Moore,
David Grecu, David Beadle, Tom Scurry,
Dan Tripoli, Jane Boegel, Kim Naves,
Mark Cookson

king of the hill

Animated Program
Deedle-Dee Productions,
Judgemental Films
& 3 Arts Entertainment
in association with
Twentieth Century Fox Television

nding

relativity

Cinematography for a Series
Michael D. O'Shea, A.S.C.

the simpsons

Animated Program
Gracie Films in association with
Twentieth Century Fox Television

Music Direction
Alf Clausen

Music and Lyrics
Alf Clausen, Ken Keeler

Sound Mixing for a Comedy Series or Special
Ron Cox, R. Russell Smith, Greg Orloff

the x-files

Drama Series
Ten Thirteen Productions in association with
Twentieth Century Fox Television

Lead Actor in a Drama Series
David Duchovny

Lead Actress in a Drama Series
Gillian Anderson

Writing in a Drama Series
Chris Carter, Vince Gilligan, John Shiban,
Frank Spotnitz

Directing in a Drama Series
James Wong

Art Direction for a Series
Graeme Murray, Gary P. Allen, Shirley Inget

Makeup for a Series
Laverne Basham, Toby Lindala

Music Composition for a Series (Dramatic Underscore)
Mark Snow

Single-Camera Picture Editing for a Series
Jim Gross

Single-Camera Picture Editing for a Series
Heather MacDougall

Sound Editing for a Series
Thierry J. Couturier, Stuart Calderon, Ira Leslie,
Maciek Malish, Debby Ruby-Winsburg,
Chris Fradkin, Jay Levine, Chris Reeves, Susan Welsh,
Jeff Charbonneau, Gary Marullo, Mike Salvetta

Sound Mixing for a Drama Series
Michael Williamson, David J. West,
Nello Torri, Harry Andronis

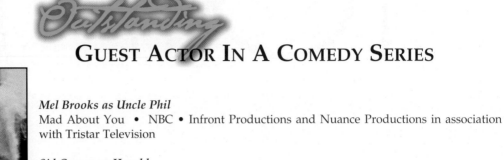

GUEST ACTOR IN A COMEDY SERIES

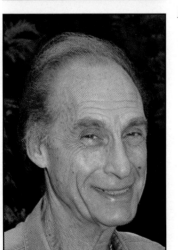

Mel Brooks as Uncle Phil
Mad About You • NBC • Infront Productions and Nuance Productions in association with Tristar Television

Sid Caesar as Harold
Mad About You • NBC • Infront Productions and Nuance Productions in association with Tristar Television

David Duchovny as Himself
The Larry Sanders Show • HBO • Brillstein/Grey Entertainment Partners with Boundaries Production

James Earl Jones as Norman
Frasier • NBC • Grub Street Productions in association with Paramount

Jerry Stiller as Frank Costanza
Seinfeld • NBC • Castle Rock Entertainment

SOUND MIXING FOR A VARIETY OR MUSIC SERIES
OR A SPECIAL

Edward J. Greene, Production Mixer; Tom Vicari, Orchestra Mixer; Robert Douglass, Re-Recording Mixer
The 69th Annual Academy Awards • ABC • Academy of Motion Picture Arts and Sciences

Don Worsham, Production/Re-Recording Mixer; Kooster McAlistar, Production Mixer
Bette Midler: Diva Las Vegas • HBO • A Miss M Production in association with Cream Cheese Films and HBO Original Programming

Gary Schultz, Rob Rapley, Production/Re-Recording Mixers
Bobby McFerrin: Loosely Mozart, The New Innovators Of Classical Music - Great Performances • PBS • Sony Classical in association with Thriteen/WNET

Edward J. Greene, Pre-Production/Production Mixer
Centennial Olympic Games: Opening Ceremonies • NBC • Don Mischer Productions

John Harris, Production Music Mixer; Andy Strauber, Production Mixer
Tony Bennett: Live By Request • A&E • Automatic Production in association with A&E Network

SOUND MIXING FOR A DRAMA SERIES

Lowell Harris, Production Mixer; Allen L. Stone, Frank Jones, Michael E. Jiron, Re-Recording Mixers
ER • Fear Of Flying • NBC • Constant <u>c</u> Productions, Amblin Television in association with Warner Bros. Television

David Platt, Production Mixer; William M. Nicholson, Thomas Meloeny, Re-Recording Mixers
Law & Order • D-Girl • NBC • Wolf Films in association with Universal Television

Joe Kenworthy, C.A.S., Production Mixer; Robert Appere, C.A.S., Ken Burton, Re-Recording Mixers
NYPD Blue • Unembraceable You • ABC • Steven Bochco Productions

Alan Bernard, Production Mixer; Christopher L. Haire, Richard Morrison, Doug Davey, Re-Recording Mixers
Star Trek: Voyager • Future's End, Part I • UPN • Star Trek: Voyager production in association with Paramount Pictures

Michael Williamson, Production Mixer; David West, Nello Torri, Harry Andronis, Re-Recording Mixers
The X-Files • Tempus Fugit • FOX • Ten Thirteen Productions in association with 20th Century Fox Television

SOUND MIXING FOR A DRAMA MINISERIES OR A SPECIAL

Larry Scharf, Production Mixer; Kevin Burns, Jon Taylor, Todd Orr, Re-Recording Mixers
Apollo 11 • Family Channel • James Manos Productions in association with MTM Enterprises, Inc.

David Lee, Production Mixer; Robert W. Glass, Jr., Ezra Dweck, Dan Wallin, Re-Recording Mixers
Gotti • HBO • A Gary Lucchesi Production in association with HBO Pictures

David Husby, Production Mixer; David E. Fluhr, C.A.S., Adam Jenkins, Don Digirolamo, Re-Recording Mixers
Titanic • Part 1 • CBS • Konigsberg-Sanitsky in association with American Zoetrope and Hallmark Entertainment

Peter Bentley, Production Mixer; Neil Brody, Bill Freesh, Mike Olman, Re-Recording Mixers
Weapons Of Mass Distraction • HBO • Massive Productions, Inc. in association with HBO Pictures

Steve C. Aaron, C.A.S., Production Mixer; Thomas J. Huth, C.A.S., Sam Black, C.A.S., John Asman, C.A.S., Re-Recording Mixers
William Faulkner's Old Man (Hallmark Hall Of Fame Presentation) • CBS • Hallmark Hall Fame Productions, Inc.

SOUND MIXING FOR A COMEDY SERIES OR A SPECIAL

Dana Mark McClure, Production Mixer; John Reiner, C.A.S., Andre Caporaso, Robert Douglass, Re-Recording Mixers
Frasier • Liar, Liar! • NBC • Grub Street Productions in association with Paramount

Klaus Landsberg, Production Mixer; Charlie McDaniel, Kathy Oldham, John Bickelhaupt, Re-Recording Mixers
Home Improvement • Wilson's World • ABC • Wind Dancer Production Group in association with Touchstone Television

Edward L. Moskowitz, C.A.S., Production Mixer; Ed Golya, C.A.S., John Bickelhaupt, Re-Recording Mixers
The Larry Sanders Show • Ellen, Or Isn't She? • HBO • Brillstein/Grey Entertainment Partners with Boundaries Production

Ron Cox, Production Mixer; R. Russell Smith, Greg Orloff, Re-Recording Mixers
The Simpsons • The Brother From Another Series • FOX • Gracie Films in association with Twentieth Television

Jesse Peck, Production Mixer; Todd Grace, Craig Porter, Re-Recording Mixers
3rd Rock From The Sun • A Nightmare On Dick Street • NBC • Carsey-Werner Productions, LLC

SYD CASSYD AWARD: THOMAS SARNOFF

Thomas Sarnoff has given generously of his time to the Academy of Television Arts and Sciences in a variety of important volunteer posts through five decades.

In 1973-74, Sarnoff was chairman of the board of trustees of the National Academy of Television Arts and Sciences. This made him eligible for the Past Presidents' Council, which he chaired for seven years, from 1985 through 1992.

Since 1990, he has served as a member of the Academy's Executive Committee. In 1990, Sarnoff also became president of the Academy Foundation, which creates and administers the Academy's educational programs.

Thomas Sarnoff is also co-chairman of the Academy's Far Sight Committee, along with *Emmy* editor and publisher Hank Rieger.

Thomas Sarnoff

Thomas Sarnoff is the scion of a distinguished broadcasting family whose members include his father, Gen. David Sarnoff, the founder of NBC, and brother Robert Sarnoff, who served as the network's president during the 1950s. But during his nearly 50 years in television broadcasting, Thomas Sarnoff has carved out an accomplished career of his own.

He has also given generously of his time to the Academy of Television Arts and Sciences in a variety of important volunteer posts through five decades. For that record of enduring service, Thomas Sarnoff is this year's winner of the Syd Cassyd Founders Award, named in honor of the Academy's founder and past president.

The award is given to an Academy member who has made significant positive impact on the Academy through their efforts and service over many years of involvement.

Sarnoff's involvement demonstrates the enduring contribution the award was created to honor. In 1973-74, Sarnoff was chairman of the board of trustees of the National Academy of Television Arts and Sciences. This made him eligible for the Past Presidents' Council, which he chaired for seven years, from 1985 through 1992. The council acted as an advisory committee to the Academy president and Board of Governors.

Since 1990, he has served as a member of the Academy's Executive Committee, which acts in lieu of the Board of Governors when Academy decisions have to be made between board meetings, and which makes decisions that do not have to go to the board. In 1990, Sarnoff also became president of the Academy Foundation, which creates and administers the Academy's educational programs.

Last year, the Foundation embarked upon a new program close to Sarnoff's heart: the Archive of American Television, a series of videotaped interviews with important figures from the medium's history. While some of the medium's pioneers have already passed on, he is nonetheless excited about helping to preserve television's past for those who will constitute its future.

As if this were not enough, Thomas Sarnoff is also co-chairman of the Academy's Far Sight Committee, along with Emmy editor and publisher Hank Rieger. Its purpose is to consider what paths the Academy may choose to take as it approaches the new millenium.

In addition to his Academy service, Sarnoff has had a long and distinguished career in television which largely parallels the history of the medium. He entered the business in 1949 as a floor manager with ABC in Los Angeles. After several quick promotions and a brief stint at MGM, he joined NBC on the west coast in 1952. Originally assistant to the director of finance and operations, he soon became director of production and business affairs (among the many deals he negotiated there: bringing the first coast-to-coast broadcast of the Emmy Awards to television in 1954.)

He was then named NBC vice president (1957); vice president, administration for the West Coast (1960); and head of NBC, West Coast. In 1965, he was elected staff executive vice president, West Coast, reporting to the president of NBC. Upon leaving the network in 1977, he founded Sarnoff International Enterprises, Inc., and in 1981, Sarnoff Entertainment Corporation, which has been active in all phases of entertainment.

But this elder statesman of the medium has never been too busy to lend a hand at the Academy. As someone who has long made his living in television, he welcomes the opportunity to give something back to the industry. He has given so much so capably for so long that he is this year's winner of the Syd Cassyd Founders Award.

Syd Cassyd Founders Award	
1991	Syd Cassyd
1992	Robert Lewine
1993	No award given
1994	Hank Rieger
1995	Larry Stewart
1996	No award given

MAIN TITLE DESIGN

Kasumi Mihori, Billy Pittard, Main Title Designers
The Burning Zone   • UPN • A Universal Television Production

Mike Jones, Main Title Designer
Dark Skies   • NBC • Bryce Zabel Productions in association with Columbia Pictures Television

Jennifer Grey, Creative Director; Earl Jenshus, Billy Pittard, Main Title Designers
Gun   • ABC • Sadwith Productions and Sandcastle V in association with Kushner-Locke

Yvonne Gensurowsky, Billy Pittard, Main Title Designers
The Learning Channel's Great Books   • TLC • The Cronkite Ward Company

Kasumi Mihori, Clark, Billy Pittard, Main Title Designers
Magical World Of Disney   • Disney Channel •

ACHIEVEMENT IN ANIMATION

(JURIED AWARD: POSSIBILITY OF ONE, MORE THAN ONE, OR NO AWARD)   THIS IS A JURIED
AWARD DETERMINED BY A PANEL OF JUDGES FROM THE ANIMATION PEER GROUP

The Emmy Goes To:

Gary Hurst, Production Designer
Testament: The Bible In Animation • Moses • HBO • Chistmas Films and S4C

Loraine Marshall, Color Director
The Willows In Winter • The Family Channel • Carlton Television in association with Hit Entertainment and The Family Channel

Phil Weinstein, Storyboard Artist
Boo To You Too! Winnie The Pooh • CBS • Walt Disney Television Animation

EMMY NOMINEES

The quest for excellence in cinematography requires extraordinary artistic talent and exceptional craftsmanship.
These cinematographers have been recognized for their achievements by
their peers in the Academy of Television Arts and Sciences. It is a remarkable accomplishment.

SERIES

JAMES BAGDONAS
CHICAGO HOPE
"A TIME TO KILL"

ROY WAGNER
GUN
"RICOCHET"

CONSTANTINE MAKRIS
LAW & ORDER
"MAD DOG"

MICHAEL D. O'SHEA, A.S.C.
RELATIVITY
"KAREN AND HER SISTERS"

JONATHAN WEST, A.S.C.
STAR TREK:
DEEP SPACE NINE
"APOCALYPSE RISING"

MINISERIES OR SPECIAL

ALAR KIVILO
GOTTI

JAMES BAGDONAS
HIDDEN IN AMERICA

FRED ELMES, A.S.C.
IN THE GLOAMING

DONALD M. MORGAN, A.S.C.
MISS EVERS' BOYS

MICHAEL D. O'SHEA, A.S.C.
*TO LOVE, HONOR,
AND DECEIVE*

INFORMATIONAL PROGRAMMING

**DON LENZER,
CHARLIE BAILEY, ANDY CIFELLI,
PETER LORCH, DAN MOYER**
ANIMAL ER

BILL MILLS
*NATIONAL GEOGRAPHIC SPECIAL;
TIGERS OF THE SNOW*

ROBERT RICHMAN
*PARADISE LOST:
THE CHILD MURDERS
AT ROBIN HOOD HILLS*

Kodak. The Filmmaker's Film Maker.

ANIMATED PROGRAM (FOR PROGRAMMING MORE THAN ONE HOUR.) AREA

AWARD: POSSIBILITY OF ONE OR NO AWARD GIVEN.

The Willows In Winter • Family Channel • Carlton Television in association with Hit Entertainment and The Family Channel
John Coates, Producer; Jonathan Peel, Executive Producer; Peter Orton, Co-Executive Producer; Dave Unwin, Director; Ted Walker, Writer

INFORMATIONAL SERIES

(AREA AWARD: POSSIBILITY OF ONE OR MORE THAN ONE AWARD.)

A&E Biography • A&E • A&E Television Network
Michael Cascio, Executive Producer; Carol Anne Dolan, Supervising Producer; Diane Ferenczi, Coordinating Producer; Peter Graves, Jack Perkins, Hosts

Discover Magazine • Discovery Channel • Produced for Discovery Communications, Inc. by Big Rock Productions in association with Blue Stone Productions, Inc.
Suzy Geller Wolf, David McKillop, Executive Producers; Evan Hadingham, Executive Producer/Writer; Mark Etkind, Producer/Director/Writer; Nancy J. Dubuc, Coordinating Producer; Daniel Levitt, Co-Producer; Peter DeMeo, Host

The Great War And The Shaping Of The 20th Century • PBS • A co-production of KCET/Los Angeles and the BBC in association with the Imperial War Museum
Blaine Baggett, Executive Producer/Writer; Jay Winter, Co-Producer/Writer; Carl Byker, Producer/Director/Writer

Inside The Actors Studio • Bravo • A Bravo Production
Jim Lipton, Executive Producer/Host; Michael Kostel, Producer; Caroline Kaplan, Series Producer; Jeff Wurtz, Director

Siskel & Ebert • Syndicated • Buena Vista Television
Larry Dieckhaus, Executive Producer; Don Dupree, Director; Andrea Gronvall, Producer; Gene Siskel, Roger Ebert, Hosts

SPECIAL VISUAL EFFECTS

(AREA AWARD: POSSIBILITY OF ONE OR MORE THAN ONE AWARD.)

Rich Helmer, Tommy Sindicich, Special Effects (Pyrotechnics); Sam Nicholson, Dan Schmit, Special Visual Effects Supervisors; Steve Melchiorre, Digital Compositing Supervisor; Jaison Stritch, Computer Graphics Supervisor; Adam Ealovega, Senior Compositing Artist; Larry Detwiler, Miniature Supervisor
Asteroid • NBC • Davis Entertainment Television in association with NBC Studios

Mike McGee, VSFX Supervisor
The Odyssey • NBC • Hallmark Entertainment in association with American Zoetrope

Gary Hutzel, Special Visual Effects Supervisor; Judy Elkins, Special Visual Effects Co-Supervisor; Paul Maples, Adrian Hurley, Visual Effects Cameramen; Don Lee, Steve Fong, Davy T. Nethercutt, Visual Effects Compositors; Kevin P. Bouchez, Laurie Resnick, Adam Howard, Visual Effects Artists; Gregory Jein, Model Maker
Star Trek: Deep Space Nine • Trials And Tribble-ations • Syndicated • Star Trek: Deep Space Nine Production in association with Paramount Pictures

Patrick Shearn, Visual Effects Supervisor; Chris Staves, Glen Bennett, Visual Effects Artists
3rd Rock From The Sun • A Nightmare On Dick Street • NBC •Carsey-Werner Productions, LLC

TECHNICAL DIRECTION/CAMERA/VIDEO FOR A SERIES

Karl Messerschmidt, Technical Director; Stephen A. Jones, Neal Carlos, Thomas Conkright, Ritch Kenney, Theodore Ashton, Camera Operators; J. A. Stuewe Prudden, Video Control
Cosby • Pilot • CBS • Bill Cosby in association with The Carsey-Werner Co., LLC

Kenneth Tamburri, Technical Director; Diane Biederbeck, Thomas Conkright, Tom Geren, Randy Gomez, Ray Gonzales, Brian Reason, Camera Operators; John Palacio, Jr., Video Control
Muppets Tonight • Sandra Bullock • ABC • Jim Henson Productions, Inc.

Steven Cimino, Technical Director; Jan Kasoff, Michael Bennett, Carl Eckett, John Pinto, Robert Reese, Camera Operators; Gregory Aull, Frank Grisanti, Video Control
Saturday Night Live • Hosted by Dana Carvey And Musical Guest Dr. Dre • NBC • Broadway Video, Inc., in association with NBC Studios

Michael Stramisky, Technical Director; Les Atkinson, Hank Geving, Rob Palmer, Kurt Tonnessen, Kevin Fraser, Camera Operators; Bill Gardhouse, Jr., Video Control
The Tonight Show With Jay Leno • Show #1079 • NBC • Big Dog Productions in association with NBC Studios, Inc.

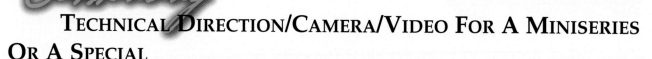

TECHNICAL DIRECTION/CAMERA/VIDEO FOR A MINISERIES OR A SPECIAL

Donna Stock, Technical Director; Wayne Orr, Ted Ashton, Rick Robinson, Camera Operators; John Palacio, Sr., Video Control
Disney's Beauty And The Beast: A Concert On Ice • CBS • Walt Disney Productions in association with Rodan Productions, Inc.

John B. Field, Technical Director; John Burdick, David Eastwood, Tom Geren, Larry Heider, Charlie Huntley, Dave Levisohn, Kenneth A. Patterson, David Plakos, Hector Ramirez, Manny Rodriguez, Ron Sheldon, Ron Smith, Camera Operators; John Palacio, Jr., Mark Sanford, Video Control
Disney's "The Hunchback Of Notre Dame" Festival Of Fun Musical Spectacular • Disney Channel • Brad Lachman Productions in association with The Disney Channel

John B. Field, Technical Director; John Burdick, David Eastwood, Helene Haviland, Charlie Huntley, Jay Millard, Lyn Noland, Bill Philbin, Hector Ramirez, Ron Sheldon, Chris Tafuri, Camera Operators; John Palacio, Sr., Susan Noll, Video Control
The Kennedy Center Honors • CBS • A George Stevens/Don Mischer Presentation for Kennedy Television Productions

David Hallmark, Technical Director; Cesar Cabreira, Wayne Getchell, Edward Nelson, Martin K. Wagner, Camera Operators; Allen Latter, Video Control
The Price Is Right 25th Anniversary Primetime Special • CBS • TPIR, LLC

Emmett Loughran, Technical Director; Charlie Huntley, Juan Barrera, John Feher, Manny Rodriguez, Jim Covello, Larry Solomon, David Smith, Ron Washburn, Camera Operators; Susan Noll, Paul C. York, Video Control
Puccini's "La Boheme" With The New York City Opera - Live From Lincoln Center • PBS • Lincoln Center for the Performing Arts, Inc.

MAKEUP FOR A SERIES

Cinzia Zanetti, Key Makeup Artist; Ron Pipes, Makeup Artist; John Vulich, Effects Makeup Creator; John Wheaton, Effects Makeup Sculptor; Mike Measimer, Effects Makeup Supervisor; Gabe De Cunto, Rob Sherwood, Liz Dean, Fionagh Cush, Effects Makeup Artists
Babylon 5 • The Summoning • Syndicated • Babylonian Productions Inc., distributed by Warner Bros. Domestic Television Distribution

Todd A. McIntosh, John Maldonado, John Wheaton, Makeup Artists; John Vulich, Effects Makeup Artist
Buffy The Vampire Slayer • Welcome To The Hellmouth • WB • Kuzui Enterprises/Sandollar Productions in association with Twentieth Century Fox Television

Camille Calvet, Michael Westmore, Karen Iverson, Ellis Burman, Steve Weber, David Quaschnick, Dean Jones, Mark Bussan, Brad Look, Belinda Bryant, James Mackinnon, Allan Apone, Perri Sorel, Mary Kay Morse, John Maldonado, Lisa Collins, Karen J. Westerfield, Makeup Artists
Star Trek: Deep Space Nine • Apocalypse Rising • Syndicated • Star Trek: Deep Space Nine Production in association with Paramount Pictures

Ron Berkeley, Key Makeup Artist; Kathy Berkeley, Makeup Artist; Thomas R. Burman, Bari Dreiband-Burman, Prosthetic Makeup Artists
Tracey Takes On... • Vegas • HBO • Takes On Productions, Inc.

Laverne Basham, Makeup Artist; Toby Lindala, Effects Makeup Artist
The X-Files • Leonard Betts • FOX • Ten Thirteen Productions in association with 20th Century Fox Television

MAKEUP FOR A MINISERIES OR A SPECIAL

Rick Stratton, Makeup Supervisor; Richard Snell, Craig Reardon, Janna Phillips, David Abbott, Edouard Henriques III, Karen J. Westerfield, Kenny Myers, Makeup Artists
Alien Nation: The Enemy Within • FOX • A Ken Johnson Production in association with National Studios

Julia Vitray, Key Makeup Artist; Anna Tesner, Noemi Czako, Eva Vyplelova, Makeup Artists; David White, Sacha Carter, Julie Wright, Prosthetic Makeup Artists
The Hunchback • TNT • Alliance Communications & TNT in association with Adelson/Baumgarten

Wynona Y. Price, Key Makeup Artist; Matthew W. Mungle, Prosthetics Makeup Artist
Miss Evers' Boys • HBO • An Anasazi Production in association with HBO NYC

Bill Corso, Makeup Supervisor; Douglas Noe, Tracey Levy, Ve Neill, Barry Koper, Ashlee Peterson, Jill Rockow, Joe Colwell, Makeup Artists; Steve Johnson, Joel Harlow, Prosthetics Makeup Artists
Stephen King's The Shining • ABC • Lakeside Productions, Inc. in association with Warner Bros. Television

Rick Stratton, Prosthetics Makeup Artist
Trilogy Of Terror II • USA • An MEC Trilogy Production in association with Wilshire Court Productions, Inc.

ACHIEVEMENT IN INFORMATIONAL PROGRAMMING

(AREA AWARD: POSSIBILITY OF ONE OR MORE THAN ONE AWARD GIVEN)

Don Lenzer, Charlie Bailey, Andy Cifelli, Peter Lorch, Dan Moyer, Cameras
Animal ER • TBS • A co-production of Turner Original Productions, Inc. and Toylsome Studio, Inc.

Bill Mills, Director of Photography
National Geographic Special: Tigers Of The Snow • NBC • National Geographic Television

Robert Richman, Director of Photography
Paradise Lost: The Child Murders At Robin Hood Hills • HBO • A Hand To Mouth Production Presented By Home Box Office

Scott Doniger, Editor
How Do You Spell God? • HBO •An HBO Production

Jason Rosenfield, Editor
Memphis PD: War On The Streets • HBO • Half-Court Pictures

Barry Nye, A.C.E., Editor
National Geographic Special: Tigers Of The Snow • NBC • National Geographic Television

Joe Berlinger, Bruce Sinofsky, M. Watanabe Milmore, Editors
Paradise Lost: The Child Murders At Robin Hood Hills • HBO • A Hand To Mouth Production Presented By Home Box Office

Vincent Stenerson, Editor
Without Pity: A Film About Abilities • HBO • Mierendorf Productions in association with HBO

Scott Reynolds, Sound Editor
A&E Biography • Judy Garland • A&E • A&E Television Network

Pattie Lorusso, Supervising Sound Editor/Sound Editor; Barry Nye, A.C.E., Sound Editor
National Geographic Special: Tigers Of The Snow • NBC • National Geographic Television

Mark McLaughlin, Production Mixer; Kent Gibson, Tom Mitchell, Alan Porzio, Re-Recording Mixers
America's Music: The Roots Of Country • Part 3 • TBS • A co-production of Turner Original Productions, Inc. and Wild Wolf Productions, Inc.

Paul Trautman, Production Mixer; Paul Schremp, Darren Barnett, Re-Recording Mixers
National Geographic Special: Tigers Of The Snow • NBC • National Geographic Television

Congratulates
the 1997
Emmy Award
Nominees

Objective. Respected. Preferred.

ANIMATED PROGRAM (FOR PROGRAMMING ONE HOUR OR LESS.)

Dexter's Laboratory • Star Spangled Sidekicks T.V. Superpals Game Over • The Cartoon Network • Hanna-Barbera Cartoons, Inc.
Sherry Gunther, Larry Huber, Executive Producers; Craig McCracken, Genndy Tartakovsky, Directors; Jason Butler Rote, Writer

Duckman • Duckman and Cornfed in Haunted Society Plumbers • USA • Klasky Csupo in association with Paramount
Everett Peck, Creative Producer; Gabor Csupo, Arlene Klasky, Ron Osborn, Jeff Reno, Executive Producers; David Misch, Executive Producer/Writer; Michael Markowitz, Supervising Producer/Writer; Gene Laufenberg, Producer/Writer; Mitch Watson, Producer; Peter Avanzino, Director

King Of The Hill • Square Peg • FOX • Deedle-Dee Productions, Judgemental Films, & 3 Arts Entertainment in association with Twentieth Century Fox Television
Greg Daniels, Mike Judge, Howard Klein, Michael Rotenberg, Executive Producers; Phil Roman, Animation Executive Producer; Joe Boucher, Richard Raynis, Producers; Jonathan Collier, Cheryl Holliday, David Zuckerman, Supervising Producers; Lolee Aries, Bill Schultz, Michael Wolf, Animation Producers; Wes Archer, Supervising Director; Gary McCarver, Director; Joe Stillman, Writer

Rugrats • Mother's Day • Nickelodeon • Klasky Csupo Inc.
Paul Demeyer, Creative Producer; Gabor Csupo, Arlene Klasky, Executive Producers; Mary Harrington, Executive Producer (Nickelodeon); Kathrin Seitz, Supervising Producer (Nickelodeon); Margo Pipkin, Eryk Casemiro, Coordinating Producers; Norton Virgien, Toni Vian, Directors; Jon Cooksey, Ali Marie Matheson, J. David Stern, David N. Weiss, Writers

The Simpsons • Homer's Phobia • FOX • Gracie Films in association with Twentieth Television
Bill Oakley, Josh Weinstein, Matt Groening, James L. Brooks, Sam Simon, Mike Scully, George Meyer, Steve Tompkins, Executive Producers; Phil Roman, Animation Executive Producer; Jonathan Collier, Ken Keeler, David S. Cohen, Richard Appel, J. Michael Mendel, Richard Raynis, David Silverman, Richard Sakai, Denise Sirkot, Colin A.B.V. Lewis, David Mirkin, Ian Maxtone-Graham, Dan McGrath, Producers; Bill Schultz, Michael Wolf, Animation Producers; Mike B. Anderson, Director; Ron Hauge, Writer

VOICE OVER PERFORMANCE

(JURIED AWARD: POSSIBILITY OF ONE, MORE THAN ONE OR NO AWARD) THIS IS A JURIED AWARD DETERMINED BY A PANEL OF JUDGES FROM THE PERFORMER AND ANIMATION PEER GROUPS.)

The Emmy Goes To:

Jeremy Iron as the voice of Siegfried Sassoon
The Great War And The Shaping Of The 20th Century • War Without End • PBS • A Co-Production of KCET/Los Angeles and the BBC in association with the Imperial War Museum

Rik Mayall as the voice of Toad
The Willows In Winter • The Family Channel • Carlton Television in association with Hit Entertainment and The Family Channel

SINGLE-CAMERA PICTURE EDITING FOR A SERIES

Alec Smight, A.C.E., Mark C. Baldwin, Augie Hess, Editors
Chicago Hope • Day Of The Rope • CBS • David E. Kelley Productions in association with 20th Century Fox

Kevin Casey, Editor
ER • Union Station • NBC • Constant c̲ Productions, Amblin Television in association with Warner Bros. Television

Randy Jon Morgan, Editor •
ER • The Long Way Around • NBC • Constant c̲ Productions, Amblin Television in association with Warner Bros. Television

David Siegel, A.C.E., Editor
Law & Order • Judgement In L.A., Part 2 • NBC • Wolf Films in association with Universal Television

Jim Gross, Editor
The X-Files • Terma • FOX • Ten Thirteen Productions in association with 20th Century Fox Television

Heather MacDougall, Editor
The X-Files • Tempus Fugit • FOX • Ten Thirteen Productions in association with 20th Century Fox Television

SINGLE-CAMERA PICTURE EDITING FOR A MINISERIES OR A SPECIAL

Tony Gibbs, A.C.E., Editor
Crime Of The Century • HBO • Astoria Productions in association with HBO Pictures

Zach Staenberg, Editor
Gotti • HBO • A Gary Lucchesi Production in association with HBO Pictures

Elena Maganini, Editor
If These Walls Could Talk • 1952 & 1974 • HBO • A Moving Pictures Production

Michael Ornstein, A.C.E., Editor
In Cold Blood • CBS • RHI Entertainment, Inc. in association with Pacific Motion Pictures

Drake Silliman, Editor
The Man Who Captured Eichmann • TNT • Butchers Run Films and The Stan Margulies Company

Michael L. Brown, Editor
Miss Evers' Boys • HBO • An Anasazi Production in association with HBO NYC

MULTI-CAMERA PICTURE EDITING FOR A SERIES

Kris Trexler, Editor
Ellen • The Puppy Episode • ABC • Black/Marlens Co. in association with Touchstone Television

Ron Volk, Editor
Frasier • To Kill A Talking Bird • NBC • Grub Street Productions in association with Paramount

Leslie Tolan, Paul Anderson, Editors
The Larry Sanders Show • My Name Is Asher Kingsley • HBO • Brillstein/Grey Entertainment Partners with Boundaries Production

Leslie Tolan, Sean Lambert, Editors
The Larry Sanders Show • Everybody Loves Larry • HBO • Brillstein/Grey Entertainment Partners with Boundaries Production

Skip Collector, Editor
Seinfeld • The Pothole • NBC • Castle Rock Entertainment

MULTI-CAMERA PICTURE EDITING FOR A MINISERIES OR A SPECIAL

Jeff U'Ren, Troy Okoniewski, Editors
Bette Midler: Diva Las Vegas • HBO • A Miss M Production in association with Cream Cheese Films and HBO Original Programming

Ron Barr, Steve Binder, Editors
Disney's Beauty And The Beast: A Concert On Ice • CBS • Walt Disney Productions in association with Rodan Productions, Inc.

Michael Polito, Editor
Happy Birthday Elizabeth: A Celebration Of Life • ABC • Gary L. Pudney in association with Tall Pony Productions for Greengrass Productions

Michael Polito, Randy Magalski, Editors; Mark Muheim, Catherine Shields, Joe Wiedenmeyer, Film Sequences Editors
The Kennedy Center Honors • CBS • A George Stevens/Don Mischer Presentation for Kennedy Television Productions

Brent Carpenter, Dylan Tichenor, Editors
Robert Altman's Jazz '34: Remembrances Of Kansas City Swing - Great Performances • PBS • Sandcastle 5 Productions and CIBY 2000 Present

INFORMATIONAL SPECIAL

(AREA AWARD: POSSIBILITY OF ONE OR MORE THAN ONE AWARD.)

Man Ray: Prophet Of The Avant-Garde • PBS • An American Masters Production/Thirteen WNET
Susan Lacy, Executive Producer; Mel Stuart, Producer/Director; Tamar Hacker, Senior Producer; William Cartwright, Co-Producer; Neil Baldwin, Writer

National Geographic Special: Tigers Of The Snow • NBC • National Geographic Television
Nicolas Noxon, Executive Producer; Mark Stouffer, Producer/Director; Kevin McCarey, Writer; Richard Kiley, Narrator

Paradise Lost: The Child Murders At Robin Hood Hills • HBO • A Hand To Mouth Production Presented By Home Box Office
Sheila Nevins, Executive Producer; Joe Berlinger, Bruce Sinofsky, Producers/Directors; Jonathan Moss, Coordinating Producer

Talked To Death • HBO • Parco International Productions, Inc. in association with HBO Original Productions
Sheila Nevins, Executive Producer; John Parson Peditto, Producer; Ellen Goosenberg Kent, Diane Rosenberg, Co-Producers; Nancy Abraham, Associate Producer; Eames Yates, Director

Taxicab Confessions III • HBO • View Film Production
Sheila Nevins, Executive Producer; Harry Gantz, Joseph Gantz, Producers/Directors

Without Pity: A Film About Abilities • HBO • Mierendorf Productions in association with HBO
Sheila Nevins, Executive Producer; Michael Mierendorf, Producer/Director/Writer; Jonathan Moss, Coordinating Producer; Christopher Reeve, Narrator

63

COSTUME DESIGN FOR A SERIES

Ruth Secord, Costume Designer
Avonlea • Woman Of Importance • Disney Channel • Sullivan Entertainment Inc. with C.B.C., The Disney Channel, Telefilm Canada

Julie Rhine, Costume Designer
The Drew Carey Show • New York And Queens • ABC • Mohawk Productions Inc., in association with Warner Bros. Television

Carolyn Grifel, Costume Designer
Remember WENN • The Diva That Wouldn't Die • American Movie Classics • The Entertainment Group/Turtleback Productions in association with American Movie Classics

Dianne Kennedy, Costume Designer
Sabrina, The Teenage Witch • Third Aunt From The Sun • ABC • Hartbreak Films & Finishing The Hat in association with Viacom Productions

Robert Blackman, Costume Designer
Star Trek: Voyager • False Profits • UPN • Star Trek: Voyager production in association with Paramount Pictures

Melina Root, Costume Designers
3rd Rock From The Sun • A Nightmare On Dick Street • NBC • Carsey-Werner Productions, LLC

COSTUME DESIGN FOR A MINISERIES OR A SPECIAL

John Bloomfield, Costume Designer
The Hunchback • TNT • Alliance Communications & TNT in association with Adelson/Baumgarten

Mary Malin, Costume Designer
The Inheritance • CBS • Alliance Communications Corp. with Cosgrove/Meurer Productions & TeleVest

Jenny Beavan, Costume Designer
Jane Austen's Emma • A&E • United Film & Television Productions for Meridian Broadcasting in association with Chestermead Ltd. and Chestermead Ltd. and A&E Network

Bob Mackie, Costume Designer
Mrs. Santa Claus • CBS • Hallmark Entertainment in association with Corymore Productions

Joe Tompkins, Jori Woodman, Costume Designers
Titanic • Part I • CBS • Konigsberg-Sanitsky in association with American Zoetrope and Hallmark Entertainment

COSTUME DESIGN FOR A VARIETY OR MUSIC PROGRAM

Ray Aghayan, Costume Designer
The 69th Annual Academy Awards • ABC • Academy of Motion Picture Arts and Sciences

Bob DeMora, Costume Designer
Bette Midler: Diva Las Vegas • HBO • A Miss M Production in association with Cream Cheese Films and HBO Original Programming

Ret Turner, Costume Designer
John F. Kennedy Center 25th Anniversary Celebration • PBS • A production of the John F. Kennedy Center for the Performing Arts in association with Smith-Hemion and WETA, Washington, D.C.

Dona Granata, Costume Designer
Robert Altman's Jazz '34: Remembrances Of Kansas City Swing - Great Performances • PBS • Sandcastle 5 Productions and CIBY 2000 Present

Jane Ruhm, Costume Designer
Tracey Takes On... • 1976 • HBO • Takes On Productions, Inc.

GUEST ACTRESS IN A COMEDY SERIES

Carol Burnett as Teresa
Mad About You • NBC • Infront Productions and Nuance Productions in association with Tristar Television

Ellen DeGeneres as Herself
The Larry Sanders Show • HBO • Brillstein/Grey Entertainment Partners with Boundaries Production

Laura Dern as Susan Richmond
Ellen • ABC • Black/Marlens Co. in association with Touchstone Television

Marsha Mason as Sherry
Frasier • NBC • Grub Street Productions in association with Paramount

Betty White as Midge Haber
Suddenly Susan • NBC • Warner Bros. Television

66

COMMERCIAL

GM EV-1-Appliances
Industrial Light & Magic, Production Company; Hal Riney & Partners, Ad Agency

HBO-Chimps
PYTKA, Production Company; BBDO, Ad Agency

Levi's-Doctor
Satellite, Production Company; Foote, Cone & Belding, Ad Agency

Levi's-Elevator Fantasy
Propaganda Films, Production Company; Foote, Cone & Belding, Ad Agency

Nike-Hello World
Joint Films, Production Company; Wieden & Kennedy, Ad Agency

CINEMATOGRAPHY FOR A SERIES

James Bagdonas, Director of Photography
Chicago Hope • A Time To Kill • CBS • David E. Kelley Productions in association with 20th Century Fox

Roy Wagner, Director of Photography
Gun • Ricochet • ABC • Sadwith Productions and Sandcastle V in association with Kushner-Locke

Constantine Makris, Director of Photography
Law & Order • Mad Dog • NBC • Wolf Films in association with Universal Television

Michael D. O'Shea, A.S.C., Director of Photography
Relativity • Karen And Her Sisters • ABC • The Bedford Falls Co. in association with the Twentieth Century Fox Television

Jonathan West, A.S.C., Director of Photography
Star Trek: Deep Space Nine • Apocalypse Rising • Syndicated • Star Trek: Deep Space Nine Production in association with Paramount Pictures

CINEMATOGRAPHY FOR A MINISERIES OR A SPECIAL

Alar Kivilo, Director of Photography
Gotti • HBO • A Gary Lucchesi Production in association with HBO Pictures

James Bagdonas, Director of Photography
Hidden In America • Showtime • A Citadel/As Is Production in association with The End Hunger Network and Fred Berner Films

Fred Elmes, A.S.C, Director of Photography
In The Gloaming • HBO • Frederick Zollo Productions in association with HBO NYC

Donald M. Morgan A.S.C., Director of Photography
Miss Evers' Boys • HBO • An Anasazi Production in association with HBO NYC

Michael D. O'Shea, A.S.C., Director of Photography
To Love, Honor, And Deceive • ABC • Robert Greenwald Productions/ABC Productions

ACADEMY'S ARCHIVE OF AMERICAN TELEVISION GROWING STRONG

Now in its second year, the ATAS Foundation's Archive of American Television continues its mission of profiling industry legends through in-depth, unedited videotaped interviews. Last year at this time, six such industry greats had been captured for posterity. The tally has now risen to 20, with another 35 to 40, among them, Imogene Coca, E.G. Marshall, Art Linkletter and Edward R. Murrow's top reporter Joseph Wershba — planned for completion by mid-December.

Those profiled in the past 12 months are not necessarily easily recognizable names, in keeping with the project's goal of presenting a unique and original perspective on television's beginnings, according to Archive executive producer Michael Rosen. Therefore, such notables as Joseph Barbera, Sid Caesar, Ralph Edwards, Don Hewitt, Hal Kanter, Delbert Mann, Martin Manulis and Betty White share the Archive limelight with Les Flory and Loren Jones, the surviving technicians who helped develop television; Ray Forrest, television's first news anchor-announcer-personality-political commentator, and Nick Stewart, the last surviving cast member of *Amos 'n' Andy*.

Studios and broadcast and cable networks have been donating funds to support the Archive, while other companies have contributed computer services and videotape stock and equipment. To make donations or offer suggestions for future interview subjects, please call the Archive's toll-free number: (888) 282-7272.

— L.S.

Congratulations to all our Emmy® Award nominees.

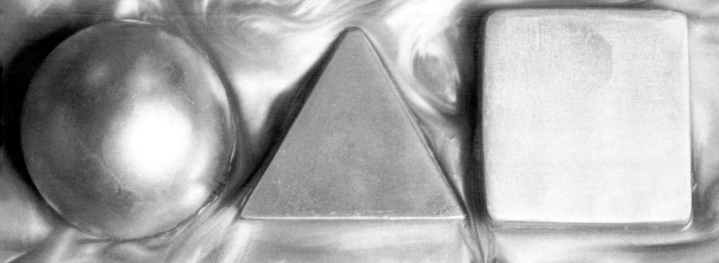

**Outstanding Lighting Direction (Electronic)
for a Comedy Series**
In The House
"The Curse of Hill House"
Art Busch, Lighting Director

Outstanding Main Title Design
The Burning Zone
Kasumi Mihori, Billy Pittard, Main Title Designers

Outstanding Sound Mixing for a Drama Series
Star: Trek Voyager
"Future's End, Part I"
Alan Bernard, Production Mixer; Christopher L. Haire, Richard
Morrison, Doug Davey, Re-Recording Mixers

Outstanding Hairstyling for a Series
Star: Trek Voyager
"Fair Trade"
Josée Normand, Key Hairstylist; Susan Bagdadi, Karen Asano Myers,
Monique De Sartre, Charlotte Gravenor, Jo An Phillips, Frank
Fontaine, Diane Pepper, Hairsylists

Outstanding Costume Design for a Series
Star: Trek Voyager
"False Profits"
Robert Blackman, Costume Designer

We're the Network, Baby!

LIGHTING DIRECTION (ELECTRONIC) FOR A COMEDY SERIES

Alan Walker, Director of Photography
Cosby • Pilot • CBS • Bill Cosby in association with The Carsey-Werner Co., LLC

Donald A. Morgan, Director of Photography
Home Improvement • I Was A Teenage Taylor • ABC • Wind Dancer Production Group in association with Touchstone Television

Art Busch, Lighting Director
In The House • The Curse Of Hill House • UPN • QDE Productions in association with NBC Studios

Peter Smokler, Director of Photography
The Larry Sanders Show • Ellen, Or Isn't She? • HBO • Brillstein/Grey Entertainment Partners with Boundaries Production

George Spiro Dibie, A.S.C., Director of Photography
Sister, Sister • The Ski Squad • WB • de Passe Entertainment

LIGHTING DIRECTION (ELECTRONIC) FOR A DRAMA SERIES, VARIETY SERIES, MINISERIES OR A SPECIAL

Peter Morse, Allen Branton, Lighting Designers
Bette Midler: Diva Las Vegas • HBO • A Miss M Production in association with Cream Cheese Films and HBO Original Programming

John C. Morgan, Robert Barnhart, Lighting Directors; Robert A. Dickinson, Lighting Designer
Centennial Olympic Games: Opening Ceremonies • NBC • Don Mischer Productions

Bill Klages, Lighting Designer
Disney's Beauty And The Beast: A Concert On Ice • CBS • Walt Disney Productions in association with Rodan Productions, Inc.

John C. Morgan, Lighting Director; Robert A. Dickinson, Lighting Designer
The 39th Annual Grammy Awards • CBS • Cossette Productions, Inc.

Gary Thorns, Lighting Director
The Tonight Show With Jay Leno • #1082 • NBC • Big Dog Productions in association with NBC Studios, Inc.

CHILDREN'S PROGRAM

(AREA AWARD: POSSIBILITY OF ONE OR MORE THAN ONE AWARD.)

About Us: The Dignity Of Children • ABC • Fred Berner Films and The Children's Dignity Project in association with Worth Associates, Inc.
Fred Berner, Debra Reynolds, Jeffrey D. Jacobs, Executive Producers; Tracy A. Mitchell, Supervising Producer; Lesley Karsten, Producer; Elaine Frontain Bryant, Associate Producer

How Do You Spell God? • HBO • An HBO Production
Sheila Nevins, Executive Producer; Carole Rosen, Senior Producer; Ellen Goosenberg Kent, Amy Schatz, Producers

It Just Takes One • USA • Ellen Weissbrod and the 7th Street Film Syndicate for USA Networks
Bonnie Hammer, Executive Producer; Ellen Weissbrod, Producer; Lorna Thomas, Co-Producer

Smoke Alarm: The Unfiltered Truth About Cigarettes • HBO • Consumer Reports Television and HBO Original Programming
Sheila Nevins, Joyce H. Newman, Executive Producers; Carole Rosen, Senior Producer; John Hoffman, Producer; Lila Corn, Coordinating Producer; Gabriella Messina, Line Producer

The Wubbulous World Of Dr. Seuss • Nickelodeon • Jim Henson Productions
Michael K. Frith, David Steven Cohen, Brian Henson, Executive Producers; Lauren Gray, Jonathan Meath, Producers; Lou Berger, Supervising Producer; David Gumpel, Co-Producer

The 48th Primetime
Emmy Awards

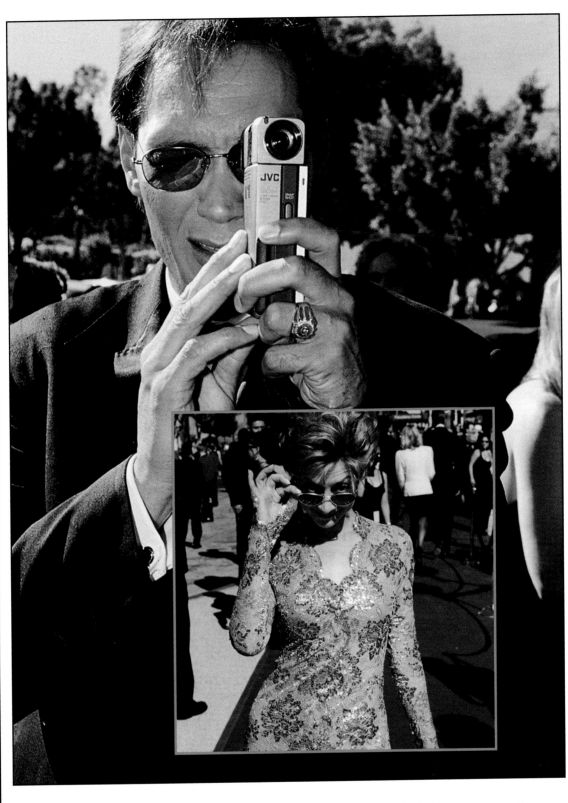

The stars were out in abundance at last year's Primetime Emmy Awards. Clockwise from above: Before the ceremony Jimmy Smits of *NYPD Blue* captured the excitement outside the Pasadena Civic with his own camcorder, while his costar Sharon Lawrence (now of her own *Fired Up)* lowered her shades for the eager photographers.

Christine Baranski of *Cybill*, always a show-stopper, did not disappoint in her body-hugging gold beads, nor, in her black cut-out gown, did *The Nanny*'s Fran Drescher, scanning the scene with Peter Marc Jacobson. Meanwhile, Matt LeBlanc and David Schwimmer displayed that familiar *Friends* brand of cool.

Host
Bryant
Gumbel

Twenty-five years ago, Bryant Gumbel began his sportscasting career right here in Los Angeles, at KNBC. Tonight he returns to mark another professional first: hosting the Primetime Emmy Awards.

In the time since 1972, of course, Gumbel has made a name for himself nationally in both the sports and news arenas. He moved up to NBC Sports in 1975, to host NFL pre-game shows. Within a few years he had become the sole host or lead anchor on NBC's coverage of major league baseball, college basketball and NFL football games. In 1980 he began reporting on sports for the network's*Today* show, and became anchor of *Today* in January 1982, a post he held until January 3 of this year. He also hosted primetime documentaries and reality-based programs, and since 1995 has hosted *Real Sports with Bryant Gumbel* for HBO. This fall he anchors the news magazine *Public Eye with Bryant Gumbel* on CBS.

Gumbel — who has won one Emmy Award for news and another two for sports: for anchoring NBC's 1988 Summer Olympics coverage; and for his HBO duties — was chosen as tonight's Emmy host at the suggestion of executive producer Don Mischer.

"Bryant is very much respected by the television community, and will help to set a tone of integrity and intelligence for this year's awards ceremony," Mischer says. "As a veteran of live television, Bryant has the ability to handle his host-ing duties with grace, charm and ease."

For his part, Gumbel says that Mischer was instrumental in assuaging his initial hesitation to accept the position. "Any time you're asked to do anything you're not known for, there is some reluctance," he explains. "I wanted to make sure I wasn't going to be asked to do something that would lessen my credibility as a television journalist. Don assured me that he wanted to take a classy, elegant look at television, and that I could help achieve that."

Gumbel may not be known for heading awards ceremonies, but he certainly knows the host's role no matter what the event. "Your job is to pass on information in as clear, concise and entertaining a fashion as possible, relieve areas of doubt, and try to make sure that the areas of down time move as fast as possible and that you get in and out of there on time," he says. As for this show in particular, "I'm fond of telling people," he says with a smile, "that this is a three-hour live broadcast and I'm very good at hosting a two-hour live broadcast."

Turning serious again, he adds, "I'm honored to be hosting the Emmys, and terribly excited. It's a different kind of show for me. We're going to have a good time."

— L.S.

Find the DIFFERENCES in these two pictures.

Look closely. Closer!
You may need to squint.
Hint: it's not *Bill Maher's*
stylish coif.

(*Answer*: This was a tough one,
but if you found the different
network logos -- you're right!)

Hey, why mess with perfection?

Your friends at *Comedy Central*

Emmy Origins

By Sandra Parker

It was the last one considered by the TV Academy, but it ended up being the best.

After rejecting 47 proposals for what was to become the Emmy statuette, Academy members in 1948 selected a design that television engineer Louis McManus had created using his wife as a model.

The statuette of a winged woman holding an atom has since become the symbol of the TV Academy's goal of supporting and uplifting the arts and sciences of television: The wings represent the muse of art; the atom the electron of science.

After selecting the design for the statuette that would reward excellence in the television industry, Academy members were faced with decision number two: What to name the symbol.

ATAS founder Syd Cassyd suggested "Ike," the nickname for the television iconoscope tube. But with a national war hero named Dwight D. "Ike" Eisenhower, Academy members thought they needed a less well-known name. Harry Lubcke, a pioneer television engineer and the third Academy president, suggested "Immy," a term commonly used for the early image orthicon camera tube. The name stuck and was later modified to Emmy, which members thought was more appropriate for a female symbol.

Each year, The R.S. Owens company in Chicago casts the approximately two hundred statuettes ordered for the primetime awards show and the three hundred for the regional awards. Although the numbers of categories rarely change, the possibility of multiple winners prompts the Academy to order extra statuettes. Surplus awards are stored for the following year's ceremony.

The statuettes weigh four and three-quarter pounds and are made of copper, nickel, silver and gold. Each one takes five and one-half hours to make and is handled with white gloves so as to leave no fingerprints.

"It's an intense process," said Noreen Prohaska, an account executive at R.S. Owens, which also makes the Oscars and trophies for other ceremonies. "They are handcast, deburred, buffed and hand polished."

The rendering of the first Emmy statuette.

WE ARE PROUD TO BE A PART OF THIS EVENING.

DonMischerProductions

To all the Emmy Award Nominees
and all the Winners...

Congratulations
on a job well done.

The Academy *of* Television Arts *&* Sciences welcomes you to the

1997

Emmy Awards

Sunday

September 14, 1997
from the
Pasadena Civic Auditorium
Pasadena, California

This evening's host
is

Bryant Gumbel

The Academy of Television Arts & Sciences
wishes to express its gratitude and
appreciation
to each of this evening's presenters

79

THE 49th ANNUAL PRIMETIME EMMY AWARDS

Executive Producer
DON MISCHER

Director
LOUIS J. HORVITZ

Writers
DIGBY DIEHL, SCOTT FIFER, BILLY GRUNDFEST,
CHRIS HENCHY, JON MACKS

Supervising Producer
MICHAEL B. SELIGMAN

Coordinating Producer
DANETTE HERMAN

Production Designers
JOHN SHAFFNER
JOE STEWART

Musical Director
TOM SCOTT

Lighting Designer
BOB DICKINSON

Nomination Film Packages
DOUGLASS M. STEWART, JR.

Special Film Clip Sequences
MICHAEL SHAPIRO

Segment Producer
GEOFF BENNETT

Production Managers
KATHY ERICKSON
DAN RUPPLE
JEFF STEMPLE

Graphics
BOB GAUTIERI

Associate Directors
JIM TANKER
DEBBIE PALACIO
MICHAEL POLITO
RITA ROGERS-BLYE

Technical Directors
KENNETH R. SHAPIRO
JOHN PRICHETT
CLIFF MIRACLE

Production Supervisor
JOHN M. BEST

Videotape Editing
MICHAEL POLITO

Staging Supervisor
THOMAS P. YOKAS

Art Director
DAVID ECKERT

Audio
ED GREENE

Assistants to Producer
JULIANE HARE
RHACHEL SHAW

Stage Managers
GARRY HOOD
RITA COSSETTE
MERV HAWKINS
HARV LEVINE
TED RAY
JASON SELIGMAN
DOUG SMITH
KEN STEIN
MARK TRAUB

Music Contractor
BILL HUGHES

Video
MARK SANFORD
STEVE BERRY

Script Supervisors
JENNIFER MISCHER
CAROL KAHL
DALE SUSAN MILLER

Senior Talent Coordinator
RICH PISANI

Videotape
RICK EDWARDS
FRED QUILLEN
REX PAULING

Production Coordinators
ALEXANDER DERVIN
LOIS CASCIO
KEVIN MEADE

Talent Coordinator
KIRSTEN ALFORD

Costumes
RET TURNER

Seating Coordinator
JUDY CHABOLA

Writer Coordinator
MAUREEN KELLY

Post Production Coordinator
TIM KETTLE

Production Staff
TANYA GARNETT
JOEY GONZALEZ
TROY MEDLEY
P. DAVID GIFFORD
JAMES COOPER
BRIAN HALL
WES THOMAS
ROBERT WOOD

Production Assistants
STEPHANIE PRESCOTT
SANDY PIERCE
MELISSA TRUEBLOOD
VANESSA IOPPOLO

Production Secretary
HEATHER MISCHER

For the Academy

RICHARD H. FRANK, *President*

JAMES L. LOPER, *Executive Director*

HERB JELLINEK, *Chief Financial and Administrative Officer*

JOHN E. GOLDHAMMER, *National Show Committee Co-Chair*

WILLIAM C. ALLEN, *Creative Arts Chair*

GEORGE A. SUNGA, *National Awards Committee Chair*

CHRIS J. COOKSON, *Engineering Committee Chair*

JOHN LEVERENCE, *Awards Director*

JULIE CARROLL SHORE, *Primetime Awards Administrator*

MURRAY WEISSMAN, *Public Relations Director*

HANK RIEGER, *Publications Director*

CARLEEN CAPPELLETTI, *Governors Ball Producer
and Special Events Supervisor*

CBS

LESLIE MOONVES, *President, CBS Television*
TERRY BOTWICK, *Vice President, Specials, CBS Entertainment*
JOSEPH ABRUZZESE, *President, Sales, CBS*
BILLY CAMPBELL, *Executive Vice President, CBS Entertainment*
NANCY TELLEM, *Executive Vice President, Business Affairs, CBS
Entertainment and Executive VP, CBS Productions*
KELLY KAHL, *Vice President, Program Planning and Scheduling,
CBS Entertainment*
GEORGE SCHWEITZER, *Executive V.P., Marketing and
Communications,CBS Television Network*
RON SCALERA, *Senior Vice President and Creative Director,
Advertising and Promotion, CBS Television Network*
BRAD CRUM, *Vice President, Affiliate Advertising, Promotion and
Network Projects, CBS Television Network*
JACK PARMETER, *Vice President, On-Air Promotion,
CBS Television Network*
KATHERINE BROYLES, *Vice President, Print Advertising,
CBS Television Network*
GIL SCHWARTZ, *Senior Vice President, Communications, CBS*
CHRIS ENDER, *Vice President, Media Relations, CBS Entertainment*
NANCY CARR, *Vice President, Publicity For Television Movies, Mini-
Series, Specials and Children's Programming, CBS Entertainment*
MADELINE PEERCE, *Vice President, Creative Services/Artist Relations,
CBS Entertainment*
MONIQUE HART, *Director, Specials, CBS Entertainment*
JIM McKAIRNES, *Director, Program Planning and Scheduling,
CBS Entertainment*

SUPPORTING ACTOR IN A COMEDY SERIES

Jason Alexander as George Costanza
Seinfeld • NBC • Castle Rock Entertainment

David Hyde Pierce as Dr. Niles Crane
Frasier • NBC • Grub Street Productions in association with Paramount

Michael Richards as Kramer
Seinfeld • NBC • Castle Rock Entertainment

Jeffrey Tambor as Hank Kingsley
The Larry Sanders Show • HBO • Brillstein/Grey Entertainment Partners with
Boundaries Production

Rip Torn as Arthur
*The Larry Sanders Show • HBO • Brillstein/Grey Entertainment Partners with Boundaries
Production*

DIRECTING FOR A COMEDY SERIES

Gil Junger, Director
Ellen • The Puppy Episode • ABC • Black/Marlens Co. in association with Touchstone Television

David Lee, Director
Frasier • To Kill A Talking Bird • NBC • Grub Street Productions in association with Paramount

Alan Myerson, Director
The Larry Sanders Show • Ellen, Or Isn't She? • HBO • Brillstein/Grey Entertainment Partners with Boundaries Production

Todd Holland, Director
The Larry Sanders Show • Everybody Loves Larry • HBO • Brillstein/Grey Entertainment Partners with Boundaries Production

Andy Ackerman, Director
Seinfeld • The Pothole • NBC • Castle Rock Entertainment

Emmy Celebrations: New York City

For the sixth consecutive year, the mayor of New York hosted a ceremony in City Hall honoring East Coast Emmy nominees. During the event, held September 3, Mayor Rudolph Giuliani presented certificates of nomination to the 1996-97 nominees who live in New York, New Jersey, Pennsylvania and Connecticut. Among those honored were Glenn Close, Bridget Fonda, Horton Foote, Peter Graves, Michael Fuchs, Meryl Streep, Frances McDormand, David Letterman, Conan O'Brien, Sam Waterston, Christopher Reeve and Dianne Wiest.

SUPPORTING ACTRESS IN A COMEDY SERIES

Christine Baranski as Maryann Thorpe
Cybill • CBS • The Carsey-Werner Company, LLC

Janeane Garofalo as Paula
The Larry Sanders Show • HBO • Brillstein/Grey Entertainment Partners with Boundaries Production

Kristen Johnston as Sally Solomon
3rd Rock From The Sun • NBC • Carsey-Werner Productions, LLC

Lisa Kudrow as Phoebe Buffay
Friends • NBC • Bright/Kauffman/Crane Productions in association with Warner Bros. Television

Julia Louis-Dreyfus as Elaine Benes
Seinfeld • NBC • Castle Rock Entertainment

WRITING FOR A COMEDY SERIES

Ellen DeGeneres, Story; Mark Driscoll, Dava Savel, Tracy Newman, Jonathan Stark, Teleplay
Ellen • The Puppy Episode • ABC • Black/Marlens Co. in association with Touchstone Television

Judd Apatow, John Markus, Teleplay/Story; Garry Shandling, Story
The Larry Sanders Show • Ellen, Or Isn't She? • HBO • Brillstein/Grey Entertainment Partners with Boundaries Production

Jon Vitti, Writer
The Larry Sanders Show • Everybody Loves Larry • HBO • Brillstein/Grey Entertainment Partners with Boundaries Production

Peter Tolan, Writer
The Larry Sanders Show • My Name Is Asher Kingsley • HBO • Brillstein/Grey Entertainment Partners with Boundaries Productions

Peter Mehlman, Jill Franklyn, Writers
Seinfeld • The Yada Yada • NBC • Castle Rock Entertainment

WRITING FOR A VARIETY OR MUSIC PROGRAM

Chris Rock, Writer
Chris Rock: Bring The Pain • HBO • Production Partners Inc. in association with HBO Original Programming

Eddie Feldmann, Supervising Writer; Dennis Miller, David Feldman, Tom Hertz, Rick Overton, Leah Krinsky, Jim Hanna, Writers
Dennis Miller Live • HBO • Happy Family Productions

Jonathan Groff, Head Writer; Tom Agna, Chris Albers, Tommy Blacha, Greg Cohen, Janine DiTullio, Michael Gordon, Brian Kiley, Ellie Barancik, Brian McCann, Conan O'Brien, Brian Reich, Andy Richter, Mike Sweeney, Writers; Robert Smigel, Writer/Additional Material
Late Night With Conan O'Brien 3rd Anniversary Show • NBC • NBC Productions

Joe Toplyn, Head Writer; Michael Barrie, Jon Beckerman, Rob Burnett, Alex Gregory, Matt Harrigan, Peter Huyck, Eric Kaplan, Tim Long, Jim Mulholland, Gerard Mulligan, Rodney Rothman, Bill Scheft, Steve Young, David Letterman, Writers
Late Show With David Letterman • CBS • Worldwide Pants Incorporated

Chris Kelly, Head Writer; Franklyn Ajaye, Scott Carter, Christopher Case Erbland, Al Franken, Jon Hotchkiss, Arianna Huffington, Hayes Jackson, Brian Jacobsmeyer, Bill Kelley, Billy Martin, Bill Maher, Ned Rice, Chris Rock, Geoff Rodkey, Michael Rotman, Jeff Stilson, Danny Vermont, Eric Weinberg, Writers
Politically Incorrect With Bill Maher • ABC/Comedy Central • Brillstein Grey Communications, HBO Downtown Productions

Tracey Ullman, Jerry Belson, Dick Clement, Ian La Frenais, Allen J. Zipper, Robert Klane, Jenji Kohan, Molly Newman, Gail Parent, Writers
Tracey Takes On... • HBO • Takes On Productions, Inc.

DIRECTING FOR A VARIETY OR MUSIC PROGRAM

Louis J. Horvitz, Director
The 69th Annual Academy Awards • ABC • Academy of Motion Picture Arts and Sciences

Marty Callner, Director
Bette Midler: Diva Las Vegas • HBO • A Miss M Production in association with Cream Cheese Films and HBO Original Programming

Don Mischer, Director
Centennial Olympic Games: Opening Ceremonies • NBC • Don Mischer Productions

Ellen Brown, Director
The Tonight Show With Jay Leno • Show #1062 • NBC • Big Dog Productions in association with NBC Studios, Inc.

Thomas Schlamme, Director
Tracey Takes On... • 1976 • HBO • Takes On Productions, Inc.

Emmy Celebrations: Los Angeles

Excellence in television was the theme of several pre-Emmy gatherings hosted for Emmy nominees by a number of professional groups.

The Kodak company hosted a dinner for Primetime cinematographer Emmy nominees on September 6 at the Bistro Garden in Studio City.

On September 9, the Directors Guild of America hosted a reception for director nominees, held at DGA headquarters in Los Angeles.

ATAS, the Screen Actors Guild and the American Federation of Television Radio Artists cohosted a cocktail reception honoring performer nominees as well as past Emmy winners. The event was held September 10 at the Westwood Marquis Hotel.

Emmy-nominated writers were feted by the Writers Guild of America West at the Beverly Hills Hotel on September 12.

PERFORMANCE IN A VARIETY OR MUSIC PROGRAM

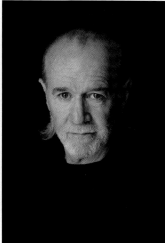

George Carlin
George Carlin: 40 Years Of Comedy • HBO • Moffitt-Lee Productions

Billy Crystal
The 69th Annual Academy Awards • ABC • Academy of Motion Picture Arts and Sciences

Bill Maher
Politically Incorrect With Bill Maher • Episode #4086 • ABC/Comedy Central • Brillstein Grey Communications, HBO Downtown Productions

Bette Midler
Bette Midler: Diva Las Vegas • HBO • A Miss M Production in association with Cream Cheese Films and HBO Original Programming

Tracey Ullman
Tracey Takes On... • Childhood • HBO • Takes On Productions, Inc.

Outstanding
SUPPORTING ACTRESS IN A DRAMA SERIES

Kim Delaney as Detective Diane Russell
NYPD Blue • ABC • Steven Bochco Productions

Laura Innes as Dr. Kerry Weaver
ER • NBC • Constant c̱ Productions, Amblin Television in association with Warner Bros. Television

CCH Pounder as Dr. Angela Hicks
ER • NBC • Constant c̱ Productions, Amblin Television in association with Warner Bros. Television

Gloria Reuben as Jeanie Boulet
ER • NBC • Constant c̱ Productions, Amblin Television in association with Warner Bros. Television

Della Reese as Tess
Touched By An Angel • CBS • CBS Productions in association with Moon Water Productions

SUPPORTING ACTOR IN A DRAMA SERIES

Adam Arkin as Dr. Aaron Shutt
Chicago Hope • CBS • David E. Kelley Productions in association with 20th Century Fox

Hector Elizondo as Dr. Phillip Watters
Chicago Hope • CBS • David E. Kelley Productions in association with 20th Century Fox

Eriq LaSalle as Dr. Peter Benton
ER • NBC • Constant c̲ Productions, Amblin Television in association with Warner Bros. Television

Nicholas Turturro as Detective James Martinez
NYPD Blue • ABC • Steven Bochco Productions

Noah Wyle as Dr. John Carter
ER • NBC • Constant c̲ Productions, Amblin Television in association with Warner Bros. Television

Outstanding
SUPPORTING ACTOR IN A MINISERIES OR A SPECIAL

Obba Babatundé as Willie Johnson
Miss Evers' Boys • HBO • An Anasazi Production in association with HBO NYC

Beau Bridges as Governor Jim Farley
The Second Civil War • HBO • Baltimore Pictures

Michael Caine as F.W. De Klerk
Mandela And De Klerk • Showtime • Showtime Presents in association with Sofronski
Productions and Hallmark Entertainment

Ossie Davis as Mr. Evers
Miss Evers' Boys • HBO • An Anasazi Production in association with HBO NYC

Joe Mantegna as Pippi De Lena
The Last Don • CBS • Konigsberg/Sanitsky Productions

89

SUPPORTING ACTRESS IN A MINISERIES OR SPECIAL

Kirstie Alley as Rose Marie
The Last Don • CBS • Konigsberg/Sanitsky Productions

Bridget Fonda as Anne
In The Gloaming • HBO • Frederick Zollo Productions in association with HBO NYC

Glenne Headly as Ruth
Bastard Out Of Carolina • Showtime • Gary Hoffman Productions, Inc.

Frances McDormand as Gus
Hidden In America • Showtime • A Citadel/As Is Production in association with The End Hunger Network and Fred Berner Films

Diana Rigg as Mrs. Danvers
Rebecca • PBS • Portman Productions for Carlton co-produced with WGBH/Boston

 Outstanding

WRITING FOR A MINISERIES OR A SPECIAL

William Nicholson, Screenplay
Crime Of The Century • HBO • Astoria Productions in association with HBO Pictures

Steve Shagan, Screenplay
Gotti • HBO • A Gary Lucchesi Production in association with HBO Pictures

Walter Bernstein, Teleplay
Miss Evers' Boys • HBO • An Anasazi Production in association with HBO NYC

Larry Gelbart, Writer
Weapons Of Mass Distraction • HBO • Massive Productions, Inc. in association with HBO Pictures

Horton Foote, Teleplay
William Faulkner's Old Man (Hallmark Hall Of Fame Presentation) • CBS • Hallmark Hall Fame Productions, Inc.

 Outstanding

DIRECTING FOR A MINISERIES OR A SPECIAL

Anjelica Huston, Director
Bastard Out Of Carolina • Showtime • Gary Hoffman Productions, Inc.

Mark Rydell, Director
Crime Of The Century • HBO • Astoria Productions in association with HBO Pictures

Robert Harmon, Director
Gotti • HBO • A Gary Lucchesi Production in association with HBO Pictures

Christopher Reeve, Director
In The Gloaming • HBO • Frederick Zollo Productions in association with HBO NYC

Andrei Konchalovsky, Director
The Odyssey • Part I & II • NBC • Hallmark Entertainment in association with American Zoetrope

VARIETY, MUSIC OR COMEDY SPECIAL

The 69th Annual Academy Awards • ABC • Academy of Motion Picture Arts and Sciences
Gil Cates, Producer

Written by Joe Bolster, Carrie Fisher, Hal Kanter, Buz Kohan
Directed by Louis J. Horvitz

Bette Midler: Diva Las Vegas • HBO • A Miss M Production in association with Cream Cheese Films and HBO Original Programming
Bette Midler, Bonnie Bruckheimer, Executive Producers; Marty Callner, Producer; Bill Brigode, Douglas C. Forbes, Randall Gladstein, Co-Producers

Written by Bruce Vilanch
Directed by Marty Callner

Chris Rock: Bring The Pain • HBO • Production Partners Inc. in association with HBO Original Programming
Chris Rock, Michael Rotenberg, Sandy Chanley, Executive Producers; Tom Bull, Producer

Written by Chris Rock
Directed by Keith Truesdell

George Carlin: 40 Years of Comedy • HBO • Moffitt-Lee Productions
John Moffitt, Pat Tourk Lee, Stu Smiley, Brenda Carlin, Executive Producers; Kimber Rickabaugh, Producer; Nancy Kurshner, Supervising Producer; Keiren Fisher, Line Producer

Written by George Carlin
Directed by Rocco Urbisci

The 50th Annual Tony Awards • CBS • Tony Awards Productions
Gary Smith, Executive Producer; Walter C. Miller, Producer; Roy A. Somlyo, Supervising Producer

Written by Thomas Meehan, Gary Smith, Bruce Vilanch
Directed by Walter C. Miller

Emmy Telecast Continues to Break World Viewing Records

Viewing records for the Emmy telecast continue to shatter each year. Tonight's show will be seen, live via satellite or more often on tape delay, by an estimated 620 million people in 90 foreign countries, up from last year's 600-million-in-85-countries tally.

For the first time ever, the United Kingdom will be tuning in to Emmy. "They have their own awards show, BAFTA—the British Academy of Film and Television Arts," explains Berle Adams, president of BAC, Inc. in Burbank, who is the foreign sales representative for ATAS. "But this year, British Sky Television has gone into buying more American programs—they have *ER*, and 11 or 12 American shows total—so it's more important to them to carry the Emmy Awards, because their shows will be nominated."

The more seasoned international participants continue to air the Emmy Awards because, Adams notes, "We tell them, 'You're part of the television industry, and you should be promoting television as an exciting form of entertainment.'" We're convinced!

—L.S.

VARIETY, MUSIC OR COMEDY SERIES

Dennis Miller Live • HBO • Happy Family Productions
Dennis Miller, Kevin C. Slattery, Executive Producers; Eddie Feldmann, Producer; Colleen Grillo, Coordinating Producer; Michele DeVoe, Associate Producer

Written by David Feldman, Eddie Feldmann, Tom Hertz, Dennis Miller
Directed by Debbie Palacio

Late Show With David Letterman • CBS • Worldwide Pants Incorporated
Rob Burnett, Executive Producer; Jon Beckerman, Supervising Producer; Barbara Gaines, Joe Toplyn, Producers

Written by Joe Toplyn, Michael Barrie, Jon Beckerman, Rob Burnett, Alex Gregory, Matt Harrigan, Peter Huyck, Eric Kaplan, Tim Long, Jim Mulholland, Gerard Mulligan, Rodney Rothman, Bill Scheft, Steve Young, David Letterman
Directed by Jerry Foley

Politically Incorrect With Bill Maher • ABC/Comedy Central • Brillstein Grey Communications, HBO Downtown Productions
Scott Carter, Nancy Geller, Bill Maher, Bernie Brillstein, Brad Grey, Marc Gurvitz, Executive Producers; Douglas M. Wilson, Senior Producer; Kevin E. Hamburger, Supervising Producer

Written by Chris Kelly, Franklyn Ajaye, Scott Carter, Christopher Case Erbland, Al Franken, Jon Hotchkiss, Arianna Huffington, Hayes Jackson, Brian Jacobsmeyer, Bill Kelley, Billy Martin, Bill Maher, Ned Rice, Chris Rock, Geoff Rodkey, Michael Rotman, Jeff Stilson, Danny Vermont, Eric Weinberg
Directed by Jessica L. Cummis

The Tonight Show With Jay Leno • NBC • Big Dog Productions in association with NBC Studios, Inc.
Debbie Vickers, Executive Producer; Patti Grant, Supervising Producer; Larry Goitia, Line Producer

Written by Jimmy Brogan, Jack Coen, Mike Colasuonno, Jay Leno, Brad Dickson, Dave Hanson, Michael Jann, Wayne Kline, Jon Macks, Anne Parker, John Romeo, Dave Rygalski, Peter Sears, Sean T. Shannon, Marvin Silbermintz, Jeffrey Spear, Marc Wilmore
Directed by Ellen Brown

Tracey Takes On... • HBO • Takes On Productions, Inc.
Allan McKeown, Tracey Ullman, Executive Producers; Dick Clement, Ian La Frenais, Supervising Producers; Carey Dietrich,Thomas Schlamme, Robert Klane, Jenji Kohan, Molly Newman, Gail Parent, Producers; Allen J. Zipper, Coordinating Producer; Stephanie Cone, Associate Producer; Jerry Belson, Consulting Producer

Written by Jerry Belson, Dick Clement, Ian La Frenais, Robert Klane, Jenji Kohan, Molly Newman, Gail Parent, Tracey Ullman, Allen J. Zipper
Directed by Don Scardino, Thomas Schlamme

AWARD

A&E Biography • A&E • A&E Television Network/H-TV Productions

ER • NBC • Constant c̲ Productions, Amblin Television in association with Warner Bros. Television

If These Walls Could Talk • HBO • A Moving Pictures Production

Miss Evers' Boys • HBO • An Anasazi Production in association with HBO NYC

Touched By An Angel • CBS • CBS Productions in association with Moon Water Productions

DIRECTING FOR A DRAMA SERIES

Tom Moore, Director
ER • Union Station • NBC • Constant c̲ Productions, Amblin Television in association with Warner Bros. Television

Rod Holcomb, Director
ER • Last Call • NBC • Constant c̲ Productions, Amblin Television in association with Warner Bros. Television

Christopher Chulack, Director
ER • Fear Of Flying • NBC • Constant c̲ Productions, Amblin Television in association with Warner Bros. Television

Mark Tinker, Director
NYPD Blue • Where's Swaldo? • ABC • Steven Bochco Productions

James Wong, Director
The X-Files • Musings Of A Cigarette Smoking Man • FOX • Ten Thirteen Productions in association with 20th Century Fox Television

WRITING FOR A DRAMA SERIES

John Wells, Writer
ER • Faith • NBC • Constant c̲ Productions, Amblin Television in association with Warner Bros. Television

Neal Baer, Writer
ER • Whose Appy Now? • NBC • Constant c̲ Productions, Amblin Television in association with Warner Bros. Television

David Milch, Stephen Gaghan, Michael R. Perry, Writers
NYPD Blue • Where's Swaldo? • ABC • Steven Bochco Productions

David Mills, Writer
NYPD Blue • Taillight's Last Gleaming • ABC • Steven Bochco Productions

Chris Carter, Vince Gilligan, John Shiban, Frank Spotnitz, Writers
The X-Files • Memento Mori • FOX • Ten Thirteen Productions in association with 20th Century Fox Television

Popular Emmy Cybercast Returns

Now in its third year, EmmyCast '97 is the official online Emmy event of the Academy of Television Arts & Sciences.

EmmyCast '97 (www.emmycast.com) features the live Internet cybercasting of both the Creative Arts Awards and Primetime Emmy Awards by utilizing digital video cameras and streaming audio/video technology. EmmyCast '97 goes behind the scenes to interview Emmy Award winners and presenters at EmmyCast Central, located in the heart of the winner's "Victory Circle." In effect, EmmyCast opens up the Pasadena Civic Auditorium to an online community of eight million web viewers as they celebrate and debate Emmy's "chosen few" in jam-packed chat rooms, post messages "in the hallway," view an Emmy photo album, and play games. Most exciting of all, web viewers can sign a virtual "Emmy-cast" for a chance to win a real plaster "Emmy-cast" worn by a member of the EmmyCast crew and signed by Primetime Award winners in attendance (make sure you sign it!).

EmmyCast '97 is produced by Ironlight Digital in conjunction with the Academy of Television Arts & Sciences. Ironlight Digital is headquartered in San Francisco with offices at the CBS Studio Center. A portion of proceeds from EmmyCast will be donated to charity.

EmmyCast would like to thank the Academy for their tremendous support and congratulate all of 1997's Emmy Award winners. We'll see you on the Internet!

LEAD ACTOR IN A MINISERIES OR SPECIAL

Armand Assante as John Gotti
Gotti • HBO • A Gary Lucchesi Production in association with HBO Pictures

Beau Bridges as Bill Januson
Hidden In America • Showtime • A Citadel/As Is Production in association with The End Hunger Network and Fred Berner Films

Robert Duvall as Adolf Eichmann
The Man Who Captured Eichmann • TNT • Butchers Run Films and The Stan Margulies Company

Laurence Fishburne as Caleb Humphries
Miss Evers' Boys • HBO • An Anasazi Production in association with HBO NYC

Sidney Poitier as Nelson Mandela
Mandela And De Klerk • Showtime • Showtime Presents in association with Sofronski Productions and Hallmark Entertainment

MINISERIES

In Cold Blood • CBS • RHI Entertainment, Inc., in association with Pacific Motion Pictures
Robert Halmi, Sr., Executive Producer; Tom Rowe, Producer

Teleplay by Benedict Fitzgerald
Directed by Jonathan Kaplan

The Last Don • CBS • Konigsberg/Sanitsky Productions
Larry Sanitsky, Frank Konigsberg, Joyce Eliason, Executive Producers; Jim Davis, Producer

Teleplay by Joyce Eliason
Based on the novel by Mario Puzu
Directed by Graeme Clifford

The Odyssey • NBC • Hallmark Entertainment in association with American Zoetrope
Robert Halmi, Sr., Francis Ford Coppola, Fred Fuch, Nicholas Meyer, Executive Producers; Dyson Lovell, Producer

Teleplay by Andrei Konchalovsky, Chris Solimine
Based on "The Odyssey" by Homer
Directed by Andrei Konchalovsky

Prime Suspect 5: Errors Of Judgement • PBS • Granada Television in co-production with WGBH/Boston
Gub Neal, Rebecca Eaton, Executive Producers; Lynn Horsford, Producer

Written by Guy Andrews
Directed by Philip Davis

Stephen King's The Shining • ABC • Lakeside Productions, Inc. in association with Warner Bros. Television
Stephen King, Executive Producer; Mark Carliner, Producer; Elliot Friedgen, Supervising Producer

Teleplay by Stephen King
Based upon the novel by Stephen King
Directed by Mick Garris

Hall of Fame Comes Home to the Academy

The Television Academy's 13th annual Hall of Fame induction, scheduled for November 1 at the Leonard H. Goldenson Theatre, will be the first in the history of the event to be held at Academy Headquarters. It is also the first induction following the conclusion of a five-year agreement between ATAS and Walt Disney World, during which time the ceremony was staged at the Florida vacation resort in 1992, 1993, 1994 and 1996, with the 1995 event held in Los Angeles at CBS Television City. This year's honorees, who were announced last month, are James L. Brooks, Garry Marshall, Diane Sawyer, Grant Tinker and posthumously, Quinn Martin. They are the Hall of Fame's 86th through 90th inductees. Following the ceremony there will be a gala reception on the Academy Plaza; with the Plaza's statues and busts of Hall of Fame members, surely no site could be more fitting.

—L.S.

Stockard Channing as Barbara Whitney
An Unexpected Family • USA • Lee Rose Productions

Glenn Close as Janet
In The Gloaming • HBO • Frederick Zollo Productions in association with HBO NYC

Helen Mirren as D.C.I. Jane Tennison
Prime Suspect 5: Errors Of Judgement • PBS • Granada Television in co-production with WGBH/Boston

Meryl Streep as Lori Reimuller
First Do No Harm • ABC • Jaffe/Braunstein Films, Ltd.

Alfre Woodard as Eunice Evers
Miss Evers' Boys • HBO • An Anasazi Production in association with HBO NYC

MADE FOR TELEVISION MOVIE

Bastard Out Of Carolina • Showtime • Gary Hoffman Productions, Inc.
Gary Hoffman, Executive Producer; Amanda Digiulio, Producer

Screenplay by Anne Meredith
Based on the Book by Dorothy Allison
Directed by Anjelica Huston

Gotti • HBO • A Gary Lucchesi Production in association with HBO Pictures
Gary Lucchesi, Executive Producer; David Coatsworth, Producer; Robert McMinn, Co-Producer

Screenplay by Steve Shagan
Based in part on the Book "Gotti: Rise and Fall" by Jerry Capeci and Gene Mustain
Directed by Robert Harmon

If These Walls Could Talk • HBO • A Moving Pictures Production
Suzanne Todd, Demi Moore, Executive Producers; Laura Greenlee, Line Producer; JJ Klein, Associate Producer

Teleplay by Nancy Savoca, Story by Pamela Wallace & Earl Wallace and Nancy Savoca (1952)
Written by Susan Nanus and Nancy Savoca (1974)
Teleplay by I. Marlene King and Nancy Savoca, Story by I. Marlene King (1996)
Directed by Nancy Savoca (1952 & 1974), Cher (1996)

In The Gloaming • HBO • Frederick Zollo Productions in association with HBO NYC
Frederick Zollo, Nicholas Paleologos, Michael Fuchs, Executive Producer; Nellie Nugiel, Producer; Bonnie Timmermann, Co-Producer

Teleplay by Will Scheffer
Based on the Story by Alice Elliott Dark
Directed by Christopher Reeve

Miss Evers' Boys • HBO • Anasazi Productions in association with HBO NYC
Robert Benedetti, Laurence Fishburne, Executive Producers; Kip Konwiser, Derek Kavanagh, Producers; Peter Stelzer, Kern Konwiser, Co-Producers

Teleplay by Walter Bernstein
Based on the Play by David Feldshuh
Directed by Joseph Sargent

LEAD ACTRESS IN A COMEDY SERIES

Ellen DeGeneres as Ellen Morgan
Ellen • ABC • Black/Marlens Co. in association with Touchstone Television

Fran Drescher as Fran Fine
The Nanny • CBS • Sternin/Fraser Ink, Inc. and High School Sweethearts in association with TriStar Television

Helen Hunt as Jamie Buchman
Mad About You • NBC • Infront Productions and Nuance Productions in association with Tristar Television

Patricia Richardson as Jill Taylor
Home Improvement • ABC • Wind Dancer Production Group in association with Touchstone Television

Cybill Shepherd as Cybill Sheriden
Cybill • CBS • The Carsey-Werner Company, LLC

LEAD ACTOR IN A COMEDY SERIES

Michael J. Fox as Michael Flaherty
Spin City • ABC • UBU Productions and Lottery Hill Entertainment in association with DreamWorks Television

Kelsey Grammer as Dr. Frasier Crane
Frasier • NBC • Grub Street Productions in association with Paramount

John Lithgow as Dick Solomon
3rd Rock From The Sun • NBC • Carsey-Werner Productions, LLC

Paul Reiser as Paul Buchman
Mad About You • NBC • Infront Productions and Nuance Productions in association with Tristar Television

Garry Shandling as Larry Sanders
The Larry Sanders Show • HBO • Brillstein/Grey Entertainment Partners with Boundaries Production

LEAD ACTRESS IN A DRAMA SERIES

Gillian Anderson as Agent Dana Scully
The X-Files • FOX • Ten Thirteen Productions in association with 20th Century Fox Television

Roma Downey as Monica
Touched By An Angel • CBS • CBS Productions in association with Moon Water Productions

Christine Lahti as Dr. Kathryn Austin
Chicago Hope • CBS • David E. Kelley Productions in association with 20th Century Fox

Julianna Margulies as Carol Hathaway
ER • NBC • Constant c Productions, Amblin Television in association with Warner Bros. Television

Sherry Stringfield as Dr. Susan Lewis
ER • NBC • Constant c Productions, Amblin Television in association with Warner Bros. Television

LEAD ACTOR IN A DRAMA SERIES

David Duchovny as Agent Fox Mulder
The X-Files • FOX • Ten Thirteen Productions in association with 20th Century Fox
Television

Anthony Edwards as Dr. Mark Greene
ER • NBC • Constant c Productions, Amblin Television in association with Warner
Bros. Television

Dennis Franz as Detective Andy Sipowicz
NYPD Blue • ABC • Steven Bochco Productions

Jimmy Smits as Detective Bobby Simone
NYPD Blue • ABC • Steven Bochco Productions

Sam Waterston as Assistant D.A. Jack McCoy
Law & Order • NBC • Wolf Films in association with Universal Television

COMEDY SERIES

Frasier • NBC • Grub Street Productions in association with Paramount
David Angell, Peter Casey, David Lee, Christopher Lloyd, Executive Producers; Chuck Ranberg, Ann Flett-Giordano, Joe Keenan, Michael B. Kaplan, Supervising Producers; Maggie Randell, William Lucas Walker, Suzanne Martin, Producers; Rob Greenberg, Mary Fukuto, Co-Producers

Created by David Angell, Peter Casey & David Lee
Based on the character "Frasier Crane" created by Glen Charles & Les Charles
Written by David Angell, Peter Casey, Dan Cohen, Anne Flett-Giordano, Rob Greenberg, Dave Hackel, Michael B. Kaplan, Joe Keenan, David Lee, Christopher Lloyd, David Lloyd, Suzanne Martin, F.J. Pratt, Chuck Ranberg, Jeffrey Richman, William Lucas Walker
Directed by James Burrows, Pamela Fryman, Joyce Gittlin, Kelsey Grammer, Gordon Hunt, David Lee, Jeff Melman

The Larry Sanders Show • HBO • Brillstein/Grey Entertainment Partners with Boundaries Productions
Garry Shandling, Brad Grey, Executive Producers; John Riggi, John Vitti, Co-Executive Producers; Becky Hartman Edwards, Carol Leifer, Supervising Producers; John Ziffren, Jeff Cesario, Producers; Todd Holland, Co-Producer; John Markus, Judd Apatow, Earl Pomerantz, Consulting Producers

Created by Garry Shandling & Dennis Klein
Written by Judd Apatow, Jeff Cesario, Becky Hartman Edwards, Maya Forbes, Carol Leifer, Lester Lewis, John Markus, John Riggi, Garry Shandling, Peter Tolan, Jon Vitti
Directed by Todd Holland, Michael Lange, Michael Lehmann, Alan Myerson, John Riggi

Mad About You • NBC • Infront Productions and Nuance Productions in association with Tristar Television
Larry Charles, Danny Jacobson, Paul Reiser, Executive Producers; Victor Levin, Richard Day, Co-Executive Producers; Helen Hunt, Bob Heath, Craig Knizek, Maria Semple, Jenji Kohan, Producers; Mary Connelly, Coordinating Producer

Created by Paul Reiser & Danny Jacobson
Written by Leslie Caveny, Larry Charles, Ron Darian, Richard Day, David Guarascio, Bob Heath, Jenji Kohan, Eric Lee, Susu Keepman Lee, Victor Levin, Moses Port, Paul Reiser, Maria Semple, Jonathan Leigh Solomon
Directed by Gordon Hunt, Michael Lembeck, David Steinberg

Seinfeld • NBC • Castle Rock Entertainment
Jerry Seinfeld, George Shapiro, Howard West, Executive Producers; Peter Mehlman, Co-Executive Producer; Alec Berg, Jeff Schaffer, Gregg Kavet, Andy Robin, Supervising Producers; Andy Ackerman, Suzy Mamann Greenberg, Tim Kaiser, Producers; Dave Mandel, Spike Feresten, Co-Producers; Nancy Sprow, Coordinating Producer; Tom Gammill, Max Pross, Consulting Producers

Created by Larry David & Jerry Seinfeld
Written by Alec Berg, Jennifer Crittenden, Tom Gammill, Spike Feresten, Darin Henry, Gregg Kavet, Steve Koren, David Mandel, Peter Mehlman, Steve O'Donnell, Dan O'Keefe, Max Pross, Andy Robin, Jeff Schaffer,
Directed by Andy Ackerman, David O'Trainer

3rd Rock From The Sun • NBC • Carsey-Werner Productions, LLC
Bonnie Turner, Terry Turner, Marcy Carsey, Tom Werner, Caryn Mandabach, Executive Producers; David Sacks, Co-Executive Producer; Bill Martin, Mike Schiff, Supervising Producers; Patrick Kienlen, Bob Kushell, Christine Zander, Producers; Mark Brazill, Consulting Producer

Created by Bonnie Turner & Terry Turner
Written by Katy Ballard, Mark Brazill, Michael Glouberman, David Goetsch, David M. Israel, Bob Kushell, Bill Martin, Gregg Mettler, Jim O'Doherty, Andrew Orenstein, Daivd Sacks, Mike Schiff, Bonnie Turner, Terry Turner, Jason Venokur, Christine Zander
Directed by Bob Berlinger, Terry Hughes

DRAMA SERIES

Chicago Hope • CBS • David E. Kelley Productions in association with 20th Century Fox
John Tinker, Bill D'Elia, Executive Producers; James C. Hart, Supervising Producer, John Heath, Rob Corn, Tim Kring, Dawn Prestwich, Nicole Yorkin, Producers

Created by David E. Kelley
Written by David Amann, Peter Berg, Ian Biederman, Joe Blake, Bob Burgos, Mary Byrd, Sara Charno, Marcelle Clemments, Tim Kring, Jennifer Levin, A. DeSantis Martin, Zachery Martin, MD, Dawn Prestwich, Josh Reims, John Tinker, Kevin Ward
Directed by Lou Antonio, Adam Arkin, Jim Bagdonas, Peter Berg, Jim Charleston, Stephen Cragg, Bill D'Elia, Jim Frawley, Jim Hart, Martha Mitchell, Michael Pressman, Michael Schultz, Oz Scott, Sandy Smolan, Jesus Trevino, Randy Zisk

ER • NBC • Constant c Productions, Amblin Television in association with Warner Bros. Television
Michael Crichton, John Wells, Lydia Woodward, Executive Producers; Carol Flint, Christopher Chulack, Co-Executive Producers; Paul Manning Supervising Producer; Penny Adams, Neal Baer, Lance Gentile, Wendy Spence, Co-Producers

Created by Michael Crichton
Written by Neal Baer, Jason Cahill, Samantha Corbin, Carol Flint, Lance Gentile, Barbara Hall, Paul Manning, Joe Sachs, John Wells, Lydia Woodward
Directed by Felix Alcala, Paris Barclay, Christopher Chulack, Davis Guggenheim, Rod Holcomb, Jonathan Kaplan, Michael Katleman, Perry Lang, Tom Moore, David Nutter, Richard Thorpe, Jacque Toberen

Law & Order • NBC • Wolf Films in association with Universal Television
Dick Wolf, Rene Balcer, Ed Sherin, Executive Producers; Ed Zuckerman, Co-Executive Producer; Arthur Forney, Gardner Stern, Supervising Producers; Jeffrey Hayes, Lewis H. Gould, Jeremy R. Littman, Billy Fox, Producers

Created by Dick Wolf
Written by Rene Balcer, Janis Diamond, Eddie Feldmann, William N. Forbes, Jeremy R. Littman, I.C. Rapoport, Barry M. Schkolnick, Gardner Stern, Richard Sweren, Shimon Wincelberg, Ed Zuckerman
Directed by Jace Alexander, Arthur W. Forney, Lewis H. Gould, Dan Karlok, Constantine Makris, Brian Mertes, Christopher Misiano, Vincent Misiano, Matthew Penn, David Platt, Ed Sherin

NYPD Blue • ABC • Steven Bochco Productions
Steven Bochco, David Milch, Mark Tinker, Executive Producer; Michael M. Robin, Co-Executive Producer; Bill Clark, Supervising Producer; Michael Watkins, Producer; Robert J. Doherty, Coordinating Producer

Created by David Milch & Steven Bochco
Written by Bill Barich, Bill Clark, Rift Fournier, Stephen Gaghan, Leonard Gardner, Hugh Levick, David Milch, David Mills, Thad Mumford, Michael R. Perry, George Putnam, Theresa Rebeck, David Shore, Meredith Stiehm, Jane Wallace, Nick Wootton
Directed by Paris Barclay, Kathy Bates, Donna Deitch, Robert J. Doherty, Davis Guggenheim, Perry Lang, Adam Nimoy, Matthew Penn, Michael M. Robin, Daniel Sackheim, Brad Silberling, Mark Tinker, Michael Watkins, Randy Zisk

The X-Files • FOX • Ten Thirteen Productions in association with 20th Century Fox Television
Chris Carter, R.W. Goodwin, Howard Gordon, Executive Producers; Joseph Patrick Finn, Rob Bowman, Kim Manners, Producers; Paul Rabwin, Frank Spotnitz, Vince Gilligan, Co-Producers; Lori Jo Nemhauser, Associate Producer; James Wong, Glen Morgan, Ken Horton, Consulting Producers

Created by Chris Carter
Written by Chris Carter, Vince Gilligan, R.W. Goodwin, Howard Gordon, David Greenwalt, Valerie Mayhew, Vivian Mayhew, Glen Morgan, John Shiban, Frank Spotnitz, James Wong
Directed by Cliff Bole, Rob Bowman, James Charleston, Tucker Gates, R.W. Goodwin, Michael Lange, Kim Manners, James Wong

Executive Producer Don Mischer.

The Television Academy welcomes back Don Mischer, serving as executive producer of the Emmy Awards tonight for the fourth time, following a year's hiatus.

Last year at this time, Mischer was recovering from the most challenging assignment he will probably ever have: creating, producing and directing the opening and closing ceremonies of the 1996 Centennial Olympic Games in Atlanta, which were viewed by 80 percent of the people on the planet. He recently undertook another mammoth task, that of producing the *Hong Kong '97 Spectacular*, a one-hour live show staged on the waters of Victoria Harbour to celebrate the tradition and culture of Hong Kong on the occasion of its July 1 handover from Great Britain to China.

With tonight's Emmy show, he is pleased to be back on what is, literally, familiar turf. "I'm so happy to be back in a theater, where we're not worried about wind, lightning, or rain," he says. "There might be earthquakes, yes — but I'll take that risk!"

Given the unique nature of the preceding two events, Mischer says that he did not really learn lessons from them which could be applied to tonight's show, but benefited in a different way. "You develop a feeling of confidence, that no matter how great the challenge or whatever obstacles might arise, there is a way of getting around them, keeping things going and making the show meaningful for people," he explains. "You want the Emmys to have some meaning, to put primetime television in a positive perspective, and to be more than just handing out awards. While big spectacles are very high profile, in some way, the Emmys are more critical, because this is our home, our community, and we care about what our peers think more than anything."

He terms the Emmy ceremony a "delicate show.

There are delicate moments, acceptance speeches, observations made. The Olympics and Hong Kong were powerful — the Olympics had a 105-piece orchestra, a 300-voice choir, a cast of over 6,000 and 25 tons of pyro, and Hong Kong had more fireworks in the air than any show, ever. So you have these powerful devices which make the audience say, 'Wow.' With the Emmys, moments are not created with powerful production, they are often unpredictable, and sometimes that makes it harder for a producer."

The specifics of those moments were still under discussion at press time, but they will include a look at the past season and at television trends present and predicted. And as always, Mischer will try to make the bestowing of awards more than routine. "In some ways this is a news show — people watch to see who's going to win," he says. "As a producer, you try to maximize this in a natural, graceful and exciting way. You try not to manipulate it."

Of course, this being a live event, there are always aspects which Mischer could not manipulate if he did try. "You try to bring together the right elements, to create humorous and emotional moments, but you never know what's going to happen," he notes. "That's part of the thrill."

He cites a "great moment" that happened at last year's ceremony (which was executive produced by Dick Clark), when Mischer's longtime colleague Louis J. Horvitz won for directing *The Kennedy Center Honors*, a show Mischer had produced with George Stevens, Jr. "Lou was in the truck, where he was directing the Emmy live broadcast as he won his first Emmy," he recalls, "so you saw him there in action. During his acceptance speech he was calling music cues and camera shots of his parents. As a producer, I love those moments, because they are so spontaneous. Everyone was cheering Lou on at that moment."

The same moment could conceivably occur tonight, as Emmy director Horvitz is nominated for directing the Academy Awards — opposite Mischer, who is nominated for his directing of the Olympics.

"We feel fine about competing against each other," Mischer says. "I'm a big fan of his. We're friends, we work together well. There's no real competition."

If Mischer does win tonight, it will prove that 13 is a lucky number. He has already been honored with a dozen Emmy Awards, as well as a record nine Directors Guild of America Awards, most recently, for his Olympics work, three NAACP Image Awards, a Peabody Award for excellence in broadcasting and Europe's prestigious Golden Rose of Montrose. He consistently chooses to produce and/or direct programs which illuminate the best of human experience, whether by spotlighting the work of acclaimed artists or by celebrating great monuments and national events. His many credits include the aforementioned *Kennedy Center Honors*, *Baryshnikov by Tharp*, *Carnegie Hall: The Grand Reopening*, *Bob Hope: The First 90 Years*, *The Tony Awards*, *Motown 25*, Michael Jackson's Super Bowl XXVII Halftime Show and several episodes of *It's Garry Shandling's Show*. On the horizon are a late-night pilot for Fox and two large-scale variety programs.

As for tonight's Emmy Awards ceremony, Mischer says, "This is a great show to do. I love being part of this evening, because we get to look at the great work that is being done on television — the great performances, comedy, and issues that have been portrayed during the season. Television promotes a dialogue on issues facing this country, and on this night, we get to take a look at that."

— L.S

107

The 24th Annual Daytime Emmy Awards

The 24th Annual Daytime Emmy Awards were bestowed in non-televised events May 17 in both New York and Los Angeles and in a televised event May 21 on ABC, hosted by Susan Lucci (*All My Children*) and Regis Philbin (*Live! with Regis and Kathie Lee*) at Radio City Music Hall in New York.

And the winners were...

TELEVISED AWARDS:

Outstanding Drama Series
General Hospital • ABC
Wendy Riche, Executive Producer; Julie Hanan Carruthers, Supervising Producer; Carol Scott, Producer; Shelley Curtis, Consulting Producer; Marty Vagts, Coordinating Producer

Outstanding Children's Series
Reading Rainbow • PBS
Twila C. Liggett, Executive Producer; Tony Buttino, Executive Producer; LeVar Burton, Executive Producer; Cecily Truett, Larry Lancit, Orly Berger Wiseman, Supervising Producers; Jill Gluckson, Senior Producer; Stacey Raider, Ronnie Krauss, Producers

Outstanding Children's Special
Elmo Saves Christmas • PBS
Nancy Kanter, Executive Producer; Karin Young Shiel, Producer

Outstanding Children's Animated Program
Animaniacs • WB
Steven Spielberg, Executive Producer; Tom Ruegger, Senior Producer/Writer; Peter Hastings, Producer/Writer; Rusty Mills, Liz Holzman, Producer/Directors; Andrea Romano, Director; Audu Paden, Director; Charles Visser, Jon McClenahan, Al Zegler, Directors; Randy Rogel, Nick Dubois, John P. McCann, Paul Rugg, Writers

Outstanding Talk Show
The Oprah Winfrey Show • SYN
Dianne Atkinson Hudson, Executive Producer; Oprah Winfrey, Supervising Producer; Alice McGee, Ellen Rakieten, LeGrande Green, Dana Newton, Supervising Senior Producers;

Kids' favorite Fred Rogers received the Lifetime Achievement Award from Tim Robbins. He was also named outstanding performer in a children's series.

David Boul, Senior Producer; Katy Murphy Davis, Angie Kraus, Producers

Outstanding Lead Actress In A Drama Series
The Young & The Restless • CBS
Jess Walton, as Jill Abbott

Outstanding Lead Actor In A Drama Series
Guiding Light • CBS
Justin Deas, as Buzz Cooper

Outstanding Supporting Actress In A Drama Series
The Young & The Restless • CBS
Michelle Stafford, as Phyllis Romalotti

Outstanding Supporting Actor In A Drama Series
The Bold & The Beautiful • CBS
Ian Buchanan, as Dr. James Warwick

Outstanding Younger Actress In A Drama Series
General Hospital • ABC
Sarah Brown, as Carly Roberts

Outstanding Younger Actor In A Drama Series
Guiding Light • CBS
Kevin Mambo, as Marcus Williams

Outstanding Performer In An Animated Program
Life With Louie • FOX
Louie Anderson, as Little Louie, Dad, Narrator

Outstanding Game Show Host
Wheel Of Fortune • SYN
Pat Sajak, Host

Outstanding Talk Show Host
The Rosie O'Donnell Show • SYN
Rosie O'Donnell, Host

© 1997 Darleen Rubin

Outstanding Drama Series Directing Team
The Young & The Restless • CBS
Heather Hill, Frank Pacelli, Mike Denney, Kathryn Foster, Directors; Betty Rothenberg, Sally McDonald, Dan Brumett, Robbin Masick Phillips, Associate Directors; Randall Hill, Donald Jacob, Stage Managers

Outstanding Drama Series Writing Team
All My Children • ABC
Agnes Nixon, Lorraine Broderick, Millee Taggart, Hal Corley, Frederick Johnson, Jeff Beldner, Christina Covino, Courtney Simon Karen L. Lewis, Elizabeth Smith, Michelle Patrick, Bettina F. Bradbury, Judith Donato, Kathleen Klein, Jane Owen Murphy, Writers

The Young & The Restless • CBS
William J. Bell, Head Writer; Kay Alden, Co-Head Writer; Jerry Birn, John F. Smith, Trent Jones, Eric Freiwald, Janice Ferri, Rex Best, Jim Houghton, Michael Minnis, Writers

Non-Televised Awards

Outstanding Game/Audience Participation Show
The Price Is Right • CBS
Bob Barker, Executive Producer; Roger Dobkowitz, Phillip Wayne-Rossi, Producers

Outstanding Special Class – Animated Program
Freakazoid • WB
Steven Spielberg, Executive Producer; Tom Ruegger, Senior Producer; Rich Arons, Producer; John P. McCann, Paul Rugg, Producer/Writers; Mitch Schauer, Producer; Ronaldo Del Carmen, Jack Heiter, Scott Jeralds, Eric Radomski, Dan Riba, Peter Shin, Directors; Andrea Romano, Voice Director

Outstanding Pre-School Children's Series
Sesame Street • PBS
Michael Loman, Executive Producer; Arlene Sherman, Yvonne Hill Ogunkoya, Producers; Carlos Dorta, Co-Producer

Home and garden diva Martha Stewart with her newest accessory.

Outstanding Service Show
Baking With Julia • PBS
Geoffrey Drummond, Executive Producer/Supervising Producer; Natan Katzman, John Potthast, Executive Producers; Bruce Franchini, Kimberly Nolan, Coordinating producers

Outstanding Special Class Program
1996 Macy's Thanksgiving Day Parade • NBC
Brad Lachman, Executive Producer; Bill Bracken, Producer; Katie Couric, Al Roker, Willard Scott, Hosts

Outstanding Performer In A Children's Series
Mister Rogers' Neighborhood • PBS
Fred Rogers, as Mister Rogers

Outstanding Performer In A Children's Special
Someone Had To Be Benny (Lifestories: Families In Crisis) • HBO
Donna Murphy, as Armanda Agrelo

Outstanding Service Show Host
Martha Stewart Living • SYN
Martha Stewart, Host

Outstanding Directing In A Game/Audience Participation Show
Wheel Of Fortune • SYN
Dick Carson, Director

Outstanding Directing In A Talk Show
The Oprah Winfrey Show • SYN
Duke Struck, Director

Outstanding Directing In A Service Show
This Old House • PBS
Russell Morash, Director

Outstanding Directing In A Children's Series
Disney Presents Bill Nye The Science Guy • PBS/SYN
Darrell Suto, Michael Gross, Erren Gottlieb, James McKenna, Directors

Outstanding Directing In A Children's Special
Someone Had To Be Benny (Lifestories: Families In Crisis) • HBO
Juan José Campanella, Director

Outstanding Special Class Directing
Sailing The World Alone • PBS
Laszlo Pal, Director

Outstanding Writing In A Children's Series
Disney Presents Bill Nye The Science Guy • PBS/SYN
Kit Boss, Erren Gottlieb, Michael Gross, James McKenna, Bill Nye, Ian Saunders, Scott Schaefer, Darrell Suto, William Sleeth, Writers

Outstanding Writing In A Children's Special
Someone Had To Be Benny (Lifestories: Families In Crisis) • HBO
Bruce Harmon, Writer

Outstanding Special Class Writing *Jeopardy!* • SYN
Terrence McDonnell, Head Writer; Steven Dorfman, Kathy Easterling, Debbie Griffin, Jeff Pierson, Frederik Pohl, IV, Steve Tamerius, Billy Wisse, Writers

Outstanding Art Direction/Set Decoration/Scenic Design
Where In Time Is Carmen Sandiego? • PBS

109

Jim Fenhagen, Erik Ulfers, Production Designers; Laura Brock, Art Director; Erik Cheripka, Hank Liebeskind, Set Decorators

Outstanding Technical Direction/Electronic Camera/Video Control
The Price Is Right • CBS
David Hallmark, Technical Director; Allen Latter, Senior Video; Cesar Cabreira, Wayne Getchell, Edward Nelson, Martin K. Wagner, Electronic Camera

The Rosie O'Donnell Show • SYN
Gregory Aull, Richard Sansevere,

Rosie O'Donnell, outstanding talker.

Technical Directors; Robert Batsche, Senior Video; Len Wechsler, Michael C. Inglesh, Ken Decker, Damien Tuffereau, Manny Gutierrez, Manny Torres, Electronic Camera

Outstanding Single Camera Photography
Reading Rainbow • PBS
Kevin Lombard, Director Of Photography

Outstanding Music Direction And Composition
Animaniacs • WB
Richard Stone, Steve Bernstein, Julie Bernstein, Composers

Outstanding Original Song

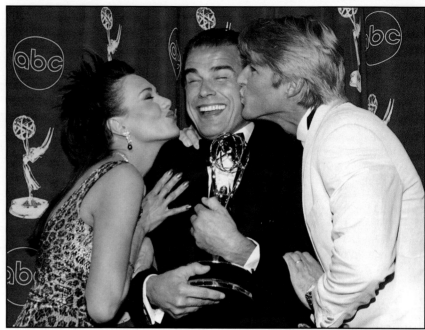

Ian Buchanan, outstanding supporting actor in a drama series, received congrats from his Bold & Beautiful *costars Hunter Tylo and Winsor Harmon.*

Guiding Light • CBS
Song Title: *Until I Was Loved By You*
Gloria Sklerov, Stan Bush, Composers/Lyricists

Outstanding Graphics And Title Design
The Oprah Winfrey Show • SYN
Thalia Kalodimos, Harriet Seitler, Title Designers

Outstanding Individual Achievement In Animation
The Lion King's Timon & Pumbaa
(Beethoven's Whiff) • CBS/SYN
Kexx Singleton, Color Director

The Magic Pearl • ABC
Barbara Schade, Background Artist

Outstanding Makeup
Leeza • NBC
Keith Crary, Anna Lujan, Judith Silverman-Orr, Makeup Artists

Outstanding Hairstyling
The Oprah Winfrey Show • SYN
Andre Walker, Hairstylist

Outstanding Multiple Camera Editing
The Oprah Winfrey Show • SYN
Michael Mabbott, John Strolia, Joseph Puglise, Editors

Outstanding Live & Direct To Tape

Sound Mixing
The Price Is Right • CBS
David Vaughn, Sound Mixer; Denise Palm Stones, Sound Effects Mixer; MaryAnn Jorgenson, Music Mixer; Jack Beller, Post-Production Mixer

Outstanding Single Camera Editing
Disney Presents Bill Nye The Science Guy • PBS/SYN
Darrell Suto, Michael Gross, Senior Editors; Felicity Oram, John Reul, Editors

Outstanding Sound Editing
Disney Presents Bill Nye The Science Guy • PBS/SYN
Thomas McGurk, Michael McAuliffe, Dave Howe, Sound Editors

Outstanding Sound Editing – Special Class
Disney's Mighty Ducks • ABC
William B. Griggs, M.P.S.E., Supervising Sound Editor; Marc Perlman, Supervising Music Editor; Paca Thomas, Supervising Sound Effects Editor; Melissa Gentry-Ellis, Sound Editor; Kris Daly, Sound Editor; Phyllis Ginter, Sound Editor; Paul Holzborn, Sound Editor; Nicolas Carr, Supervising Music Editor; Jeff Hutchins, Sound Effects Editor; Ken D. Young, Sound Effects Editor; Bill

Continued on page 112

A little night magic

We are honored tonight to celebrate our twentieth consecutive year as the home of the EMMY Awards. We've been working late all summer long to help create the magic that such an important occasion deserves.

We welcome and congratulate the best of the incredible artists who create the televised magic enjoyed by millions each year. It is only fitting that you are the very first guests to enjoy our newly renovated and restored Pasadena Civic Auditorium.

Thank you for being here to share in the magic of tonight's festivities in this special theatre. We hope to see you again for many more nights of magic.

THE PASADENA CIVIC

Command the Best.

Continued from page 110
Kean, M.P.S.E., Sound Effects Editor;
David Lynch, Sound Effects Editor;
Otis Van Osten, Sound Effects Editor;
Jennifer E. Mertens, Sound Editor;
Eric Hertsgaard, Sound Editor

Outstanding Sound Mixing
Flipper • SYN
Jon Taylor, Kevin Burns, Todd Orr,
Re-Recording Mixers; Craig
Walmsley, Production Mixer
**Outstanding Sound Mixing –
Special Class**
The Lion King's Timon & Pumbaa •
CBS/SYN
James C. Hodson, Melissa Gentry-
Ellis, Michael Beiriger, Daniel Hiland,
Joseph Citarella, Allen L. Stone,
Michael Jiron, Re-Recording Mixers;
Deb Adair, Production Mixer

Outstanding Lighting Direction
*Secrets Of The Cryptkeeper's Haunted
House* • CBS
Carl Gibson, Lighting Director

**Outstanding Costume
Design/Styling**
Educating Mom (ABC Afterschool Special)
• ABC
Durinda Wood, Costume Designer

Elmo Saves Christmas • PBS
Bill Kellard, Terry Roberson,
Costume Designers; Ed Christie,
Mark Zeszotek, Lara Maclean,
Stephen Rotondaro, Carlo Yannuzzi,
Muppet Costume Designers

**Outstanding Art Direction/Set
Decoration/Scenic Design For A
Drama Series**
Days Of Our Lives • NBC
Chip Dox, Production Designer;Wade
Battley, Art Director; Tom Early,
Sheree Miller, Lance Zeck, Steve
Nibbe, Set Decorators

The Young & The Restless • CBS
Bill Hultstrom, Production Designer;
David Hoffmann, Norman Wadell,
Art Directors; Joe Bevacqua, Fred
Cooper, Andrea Joel, Set Decorators

**Outstanding Technical
Direction/Electronic Camera/Video
Control For A Drama Series**

*Louie Anderson captured the Daytime Emmy for outstanding performer in an animat-
ed program for his multi-voiced work on* Life with Louie.

The Young & The Restless • CBS
Janice L. Bendiksen, Jim Dray, Donna
Stock, Technical Directors; John
Bromberek, Sandra Harris, Dean
Lamont, Tracy J. Lawrence, Sheldon
Mooney, Electronic Camera
Operators; Roberto Bosio, Scha Jani,
Senior Video

**Outstanding Music Direction And
Composition For A Drama Series**
Days Of Our Lives • NBC
Ken Corday, D. Brent Nelson,
Dominic Messinger, Cory Lerios,
John D'Andrea, Composers; Amy
Burkhard Evans, Stephen Reinhardt,
Music Supervisors

**Outstanding Makeup For A Drama
Series**
Days Of Our Lives • NBC
Gail J. Hopkins, Nina Wells, Corina
C. Duran, Joleen Rizzo, Gail
Brubaker, Makeup Artists

**Outstanding Hairstyling For A
Drama Series**
Days Of Our Lives • NBC
Terrie Velazquez, Hairstylist
Tom Real, Hairstylist
Natascha Ladek, Hairstylist

**Outstanding Multiple Camera
Editing For A Drama Series**

The Young & The Restless • CBS
The Bold & The Beautiful • CBS
Jim Jewell, Fred Rodey, Editors

**Outstanding Live & Direct To Tape
Sound Mixing For A Drama Series**
General Hospital • ABC
Terry Fountain, Jan Hoag, Sound
Mixers; Gary Bressler, Music Mixer;
Sylvia Almstadt, Willie Earl, Fred
Fryrear, Paulette Cronkhite, Christina
Tyson, Boom Operators; Sandy
Masone, Sound Effects Mixer; Donald
Smith, Fritz Curtis, Steve Burch, Post-
Production Mixers

**Outstanding Lighting Direction For
A Drama Series**
The Young & The Restless • CBS
William Roberts, Ray Thompson,
Rudolph Hunter, Rod Yamane,
Lighting Directors

**Outstanding Costume Design For A
Drama Series**
General Hospital • ABC
Bob Miller, Steve Howard, Costume
Designers

The Television Academy extends its
warmest congratulations to all the
winners of the 24th Annual Daytime
Emmy Awards.

PINKERTON

CONGRATULATES

ALL OF THE

1997

EMMY

AWARD

NOMINEES.

WE ARE

HONORED

TO PROVIDE

SECURITY

SERVICES

FOR THE

ANNUAL

EMMY

AWARDS.

For information on

Pinkerton's domestic or

international services

call 800-232-7465.

Fax: 800-984-4100

Web site: www.pinkertons.com

Charles F. Jenkens

Lifetime Achievement Award Recipient :

Richard E. Wiley

At first glance it might seem unusual for the Television Academy to honor an attorney with the Charles F. Jenkins Lifetime Achievement Award. After all, this top engineering award is named for the inventor of the forerunner of television, and is given to a living person whose contributions over a long period of time have significantly affected the state of television technology and engineering.

But when the attorney is Richard E. Wiley, such recognition is unquestionably merited. For when not accruing billable hours, the former Federal Communications Commission Chairman spent nine years (1987-1996) in what he terms a "labor of love:" serving as the Chairman of the FCC Advisory Committee on Advanced Television Service, which developed the standard for digital television. Incorporating high definition television for crystal clear picture and sound, the flexibility to switch from that mode to standard definition and the capability of inter-operating with other imaging media devices such as computers, digital television marks the greatest change in television technology since its invention and subsequent colorization. (The last time television standards were set, by the National Televisions Systems Committee, was 1941.)

As the guiding force of the advisory committee, Wiley oversaw the reduction of the initial 23 systems manufacturers to seven, then persuaded those seven to work together as a Grand Alliance rather than

Richard E. Wiley with his statuette.

Continued on page 116

Lucent Technologies
Bell Labs Innovations

MIT

NEX^{LEVEL}™

PHILIPS

SARNOFF
Corporation

THOMSON

zenith

*T*he
members of the
Digital HDTV Grand Alliance,
proud recipients of a
Primetime Engineering Emmy,
wish to thank the
Academy of Television Arts & Sciences
for honoring us
with this prestigious award.
Our technology, upon which
the new U.S. standard for
digital TV broadcasting
is based, redefines the
medium of television
for the 21st century.

See you on the
digital frontier.

Continued from page 114

compete against each other. The Grand Alliance members — Lucent Technologies, Sarnoff Corporation, General Instrument, Massachusetts Institute of Technology, Philips Research, Thomson Consumer Electronics and Zenith — received Engineering Emmy Awards this year. The first digital television sets will make their debut at the Consumer Electronics Show in Las Vegas early next year, and will be available to consumers mid-year.

Though he began his career as an anti-trust lawyer in Chicago, Wiley has worked in the communications field since 1970, when then-FCC Chairman Dean Burch hired him as FCC general counsel. He was appointed a commissioner two years later, moving up to Chairman in 1974. Upon leaving the FCC in 1977, he practiced communications law in Washington D.C., and in 1983 founded his own firm there, Wiley, Rein & Fielding. With more than 50 of its nearly 200 lawyers specializing in communications, the firm is the country's largest in communications practice.

During his FCC tenure, Wiley was instrumental in the agency's initial efforts to encourage increased competition and lessened regulation in the communications field. In his private practice, he has helped clients introduce products and services for FCC approval, such as securing the first license for the first direct broadcast service.

Wiley's presentation was the highlight of this year's Emmy statuettes and plaques for engineering presented July 10 at a ceremony at the Beverly Hills Hotel which drew about 150 people. ATAS Executive Director Dr. James L. Loper opened the ceremony and introduced ATAS President Rich Frank, who explained the importance of the Engineering Awards and how they are determined.

Engineering Award Committee chair Chris Cookson then bestowed the honors.

Wiley's acceptance of the Jenkins Award drew a standing ovation.

Wiley is a member of Broadcasting & Cable magazine's Hall of Fame and has served as President of the Federal Bar and Federal Communications Bar Associations. He was the 1996 recipient of the Electronic Industries Association's Medal of Honor for his work as FCC Advisory Committee Chairman. He is currently Chair of the Advisory Board of Columbia University's Institute for Tele-Information.

— L.S

The 1997 Engineering Awards presentation of statuette and plaques was held at a July 10th ceremony at the Beverly Hills Hotel.

CHARLES F. JENKINS LIFETIME ACHIEVEMENT AWARD RECIPIENTS

1991	Harry Lubcke
1992	Kerns H. Powers
1993	Richard S. O'Brien
1994	No award given
1995	Julius Barnathan
1996	No award given

1997 ENGINEERING AWARD WINNERS

Emmy statuette to Richard E. Wiley for the Charles F. Jenkins Lifetime Achievement Award
Emmy statuette to the Grand Alliance: Lucent Technologies, Sarnoff Corporation, General Instrument, Massachusetts Institute of Technology, Philips Research, Thomson Consumer Electronics, Zenith for the Grand Alliance Digital TV Standard
Emmy statuette to Video Systems Division, AVC Company, Matsushita Electric Industrial Co. Ltd. for the Panasonic AJ-LT75 DVCPRO Laptop Editor
Emmy statuette to J.L. Fisher, Inc. for J.L. Fisher Camera Dollies
Engineering plaque to Grant Loucks, Bob Kuhagen and Sid Spaldingfor the Mark V Director's Viewfinder
Engineering plaque to Bruce Arledge, Jr. for the BOOM TRAC (tm) Microphone Dolly System

For the Academy

JAMES L. LOPER
Executive Director

GLYNISS ANTHONY
Executive Assistant

AWARDS

JOHN LEVERENCE
Director

JULIE CARROLL SHORE
Primetime Administrator

BARBARA CHASE
Daytime Awards Director

LOUISE P. DANTON
L.A. Area Administrator

SHERI EBNER
Awards Coordinator

TRACY MEDEIROS
Awards Associate

JULIE COFFEY
Awards Assistant

MEMBERSHIP AND ACTIVITIES

LINDA J. LOE
Director

ROBERT O'DONNELL
Activities Administrator

DINA SARAGOSA
Membership Administrator

MARY PARRILLO
Assistant to the Director

MYEVA FOX
Membership Assistant

EDUCATIONAL PROGRAMS AND SERVICES

PRICE HICKS
Director

MURIEL CAHN
Administrator

STEPHANIE MOFFETT HYNDS
Programs Coordinator

And thanks to our very special
part-time staff:
Zac Nelson

BUSINESS AND ADMINISTRATIVE

HERB JELLINEK
Chief Financial and Administrative Officer

LISA FIKE
Controller

NORA TYREE
Staff Accountant

JEANNE ORTIZ
Assistant to the CFO

VERONICA ROSALES
Staff Accountant

HENRY MAGALLON
Manager, Information
Systems/Webmaster

CHARLES SOWELL
Office & Facilities Manager

JIMMIE JACKSON
Facilities & Office Assistant

CRAIG RUBIO
Facilities & Office Assistant

NICOLE DUFFY
Receptionist

JOHN YINGLING
Manager, Theatre Operations

VICKY CAMPOBASSO
Theatre Administrator

SPECIAL EVENTS
CARLEEN CAPPELLETTI
Supervisor

49TH PRIMETIME EMMY AWARDS PROGRAM

DONNA FREIERMUTH
Editor

CHARLES DICKENS PHILLIPS
Art Director

JULIE CARROLL SHORE
Awards Editor

KATHLEEN O'STEEN
Associate Editor

JOHN P. MCCARTHY
Director of Advertising

JOHN LEVERENCE AND HANK RIEGER
Publishers

EMMY MAGAZINE

HANK RIEGER
Editor and Publisher

GAIL POLEVOI
Managing Editor

KATHLEEN O'STEEN
Associate Editor

CHARLES DICKENS PHILLIPS
Art Director

JOHN P. MCCARTHY
Advertising Director

PETER UHRY
East Coast Advertising

ROSA M. MADONNA
Administrative Assistant

Archive of American Television
MICHAEL ROSEN
Executive Producer

SUNNY PARICH
Assistant to the Executive Producer

ERNST & YOUNG, LLP
Independent Auditors and
Ballot Tabulation

MURRAY WEISSMAN & ASSOCIATES
Public Relations

DIXON Q. DERN, ESQ.
Legal Counsel

RAY MCLIN, LAWRENCE HESS
Security

117

119

CREATIVE ARTS SHOW COMMITTEE

BILL ALLEN
Chair

MEMBERSHIP COMMITTEE

GERIANN GERACI
Chair

CONRAD G. BACHMANN
CLIFFORD DEKTAR
HAL EISNER

TERESA KOENIG
SHEILA MANNING

LEE MILLER
SHERMAN L. THOMPSON
PATRICIA VAN RYKER

STAFF MEMBER: LINDA J. LOE

BYLAWS COMMITTEE

HANK RIEGER
Chair
Deborah Miller
Vice Chair

CONRAD G. BACHMANN
BETH BOHN

DIXON Q. DERN
JAMES L. LOPER

JAN SCOTT
NANCY B. WIARD

STAFF MEMBER: LINDA J. LOE

AUDIT & FINANCE COMMITTEE

EDWARD A. ROMANO
Chair

VICKI N. GABOR
REGINALD G. HARPUR

MERYL C. MARSHALL
ELIZABETH L. WU

STAFF MEMBER: HERB JELLINEK

FAR SIGHT COMMITTEE

HANK RIEGER
THOMAS W. SARNOFF
Co-Chairs

LOREEN ARBUS
STUART H. BERG
LEO CHALOUKIAN
JEFFREY I. COLE
J. PATRICK COLLINS

DIXON Q. DERN
ROBERT S. FINKEL
SONNY FOX
RICHARD H. FRANK
JAMES L. LOPER
MERYL C. MARSHALL

JOHN NACHREINER
JAN SCOTT
SUSAN A. SIMONS
DON TILLMAN
NANCY B. WIARD

STAFF MEMBER: LINDA J. LOE

Daytime Awards Committee

NANCY BRADLEY WIARD
Chair
DAVID MICHAELS
Vice-Chair

RAY ANGONA
BARBARA BLOOM
ROBERT BODEN
KERRY L. BROOM
THOMAS C. CAMPBELL
ROCCI CHATFIELD
CHIP DOX
RICHARD H. FRANK
PAUL FRAZIER

GAIL J. HOPKINS
JAMES HOUGHTON
BARBARA HUNTER
JOHN INGLE
ANNAMARIE KOSTURA
SUSAN D. LEE
DARLENE LIEBLICH
JAMES L. LOPER

LINDA MANCUSO
GREGORY MENG
BOB MILLER
MERYL O'LOUGHLIN
WENDY RICHE
SUSAN A. SIMONS
HOPE H. SMITH
DAN WEAVER
JOHN C. ZAK

STAFF MEMBER: BARBARA CHASE

Daytime Show Committee

SUSAN A. SIMONS
Chair

L.A. Area Awards Committee

HAL EISNER
SOCORRO SERRANO
Co-Chairs

DON TILLMAN
VICE PRESIDENT, L.A.

JOANIE BECKER
LISA BROWN
MARYHELEN CAMPA
JOYCE CAMPBELL
BERTHA CASTRO
TONY CATENACCI
LAURA CONTRERAS
ROBIN GEE
MARIA GUTIERREZ
HARRY KOOPERSTEIN

VELIA LaGARDA
FERNANDO LOPEZ
CHRISTIE LUGO
DEREK MALDONADO
JAIRO MARIN
MILLI MARTINEZ
CAROL MYERS MARTZ
MICHELLE MERKER
LILIA MONTES
STEPHANIE MOORE
SUSAN NAKAMURA

PETER O'CONNELL
HECTOR PASILLAS
JOE QUASARANO
TOM SEARSON
ROBERTA SMITH
SYLVIA TEAGUE
SABRINA FAIR THOMAS
MITCH WALDOW
STEPHANIE ZAITA
VAL ZAVALA

STAFF MEMBER: LOUISE P. DANTON

Engineering Awards Committee

CHRIS J. COOKSON
Chair

ROBERT FABER
ALAN A. HART

ROBERT K. LAMBERT
BARRY ZEGEL

STAFF MEMBER: JOHN LEVERENCE

Governors Award Nominating Committee

MERYL C. MARSHALL
Chair

JANET ASHIKAGA
ROBERT BODEN

GERIANN GERACI
TERESA KOENIG

DEBORAH MILLER
LEE MILLER

STAFF MEMBER: BARBARA CHASE, JOHN LEVERENCE

121

Hall Of Fame Selection Committee

EDGAR J. SCHERICK
Chair

DANIEL H. BLATT
STEVEN BOCHCO

CARLEEN CAPPELLETTI
SUZANNE dE PASSE
RICHARD H. FRANK

DAVID GERBER
JAMES L. LOPER

Hall Of Fame Show Committee

GEORGE A. SUNGA
Chair

Hall Of Fame Sculpture Committee

RICHARD STILES
Chair

RENE LAGLER
SYDNEY Z. LITWACK

JAMES L. LOPER
JAN SCOTT

Activities Advisory Committee

JAMES L. LOPER
Chair

RAY ANGONA
CONRAD G. BACHMANN
DANIEL H. BIRMAN
BETH BOHN
TERRY A. BOTWICK
DAVID BLAKE CHATFIELD
ROCCI CHATFIELD
JEFFREY I. COLE

GEORGE DAUGHERTY
CLIFFORD DEKTAR
MAURA R. DUNBAR
DAN EINSTEIN
GERIANN GERACI
SHERI GOLDBERG
MICHAEL A. HOEY, A.C.E.
PAULA L. KAATZ
SHEILA MANNING

IRENE NACHREINER
JOHN NACHREINER
MERYL O'LOUGHLIN
HANK RIEGER
JULES F. SIMON
DON TILLMAN
LANCE WEBSTER
MURRAY WEISSMAN

STAFF MEMBERS: LINDA J. LOE, ROBERT O'DONNELL

Future Media Committee

MEDORA HEILBRON
MATHEW J. TOMBERS
Co-Chairs

DAVID BARON
BETH BOHN
PAUL BRICAULT
PETER CALABRESE
BOB CHMIEL

JEFFREY I. COLE
MAURA R. DUNBAR
STUART H. FOX
MEDORA HEILBRON

LUCY A. HOOD
MONIA B. JOBLIN
BETH B. KENNEDY
ROBERT H. LEVI
MERYL C. MARSHALL

Past Presidents Council

SONNY FOX
Chair

ALAN A. ARMER
RICHARD J. BERG
SYD CASSYD
LEO CHALOUKIAN

DOUGLAS M. DUITSMAN
RICHARD H. FRANK
JOHN GUEDEL
SERGE KRIZMAN
DAVID LAWRENCE

DIANA MULDAUR
HANK RIEGER
THOMAS W. SARNOFF
MIKE STOKEY

EDUCATIONAL PROGRAMS & SERVICES COMMITTEE

MICHAEL O. GALLANT
Chair
NANCY MEYER
Vice-Chair

DAVID L. BELL	STEPHEN R. FISCH	KENNETH HARWOOD
BARRY R. BERNSON	ANN L. GIBBS	JOEL HELLER
BRUCE BILSON	GARY G. GOLDBERGER	DAVID HOROWITZ
DANIEL H. BIRMAN	SHARI GOODHARTZ	LEW HUNTER
MICHAEL BLOEBAUM	STEVE GORDON	NANCI LINKE-ELLIS
KAREN LEE COPELAND	JOHN F. GREGORY	DAMON E. ROMINE
IVAN N. CURY	ANNAMARIE GRIFFIN	ERIC STEIN
RICHARD EISBROUCH	LYNNE S. GROSS	GEORGE STELZNER
PHILLIP ESSMAN		VICTORIA STERLING

STAFF MEMBERS: PRICE HICKS, MURIEL CAHN, STEPHANIE MOFFETT HYNDS

PUBLIC RELATIONS COMMITTEE

DON DEMESQUITA
Chair

DON ADAMS	DAN DORAN	DALE C. OLSON
STUART H. BERG	CHRIS ENDER	CHARLES A. PANAMA
SHERRIE BERGER	ROSA GATTI	RUSS L. PATRICK
SUE BINFORD	LIBBY GILL	JUSTIN PIERCE
HENRI BOLLINGER	SHERI GOLDBERG	KIM REED
JIM BOYLE	SUZANNE GORDON	HANK RIEGER
KEVIN M. BROCKMAN	KATHLEEN GRAHAM	MARK ROSCH
BARBARA S. BROGLIATTI	ALISON LOUISE HILL	CINDY RONZONI
SCOTT BROYLES	CHRISTINA KOUNELIAS	LES SCHECTER
NANCY CARR	EILEEN KURTZ	HEIDI A. TROTTA
TERRI CORIGLIANO	NANCY LESSER	LANCE WEBSTER
CLIFFORD DEKTAR	CRAIG MARTINELLI	MURRAY WEISSMAN
MARCY DEVEAUX	ROBIN MCMILLAN	JOHN WENTWORTH
	STEVEN MELNICK	ROBERT WERDEN

AD HOC EMMY TELECAST PUBLIC RELATIONS COMMITTEE

MURRAY WEISSMAN
Chair

DON ADAMS	PAUL GENDREAU	CRAIG MARTINELLI
STUART H. BERG	LIBBY GILL	JOANNA DODD MASSEY
SHERRIE BERGER	SHERI GOLDBERG	DALE C. OLSON
HENRI BOLLINGER	SUZANNE GORDON	HANK RIEGER
NANCY CARR	KATHLEEN GRAHAM	MARK ROSCH
CLIFFORD DEKTAR	ALISON LOUISE HILL	LES SCHECTER
DICK DELSON	MARK KERN	HEIDI A. TROTTA
DON DEMESQUITA	EILEEN KURTZ	CHUCK WARN
DAN DORAN	MARVIN LEVY	LANCE WEBSTER
JOSEPH B. EARLEY	SHARAN MAGNUSON	MURRAY WEISSMAN
CHRIS ENDER		ROBERT WERDEN

123

TV CARES: ATAS FIGHTS AIDS COMMITTEE

DAVID MICHAELS
Chair
ANGELA LANSBURY
Honorary Chair

JASON ALEXANDER
KAREN ANGONA NOLAN
JUNE M. BALDWIN
SCOTT BARTON
LEE PHILLIP BELL
BARBARA ALLYNE BENNET
ROBERT BERGER
PETER BERGMAN
B. HARLAN BOLL
JANICE D. BRANDOW
TIMOTHY STEPHEN BRAUN
BARBARA CHASE
JOYCE COLEMAN
DARLENE CONLEY

JEANNE COOPER
JONATHAN DOWNING
STEVE ENG
BRENDA FELDMAN
LISA FIKE
SUSAN FINCHAM
LEEZA GIBBONS
FLORENCE HENDERSON
JOHN INGLE
MARK ALLEN ITKIN
LUCY JOHNSON
PAULA L. KAATZ
KELLY LANGE
ANGELA LANSBURY
VICKI LAWRENCE
DARLENE LIEBLICH

KATE LINDER
LINDA J. LOE
JAMES L. LOPER
PEGGY MCCAY
JOAN MESSINGER
DEBORAH MILLER
NICK MOENSSENS
JOSHUA MORROW
MELODY THOMAS SCOTT
SUSAN A. SIMONS
ELIZABETH F. SUNG
MICHAEL SUTTON
LIZ TORRES
NANCY B. WIARD
JOHN C. ZAK

50TH ANNIVERSARY COMMITTEE

HANK RIEGER
LARRY STEWART*
Co-Chair
SYD CASSYD
Honorary Chair

DON ADAMS
JEANENE AMBLER, A.C.E.
RAY ANGONA
PADMA ATLURI
CONRAD G. BACHMANN
BRIAN C. BARTHOLOMEW
RICHARD R. BELLIS
JON BURLINGAME
CARLEEN CAPPELLETTI
JAMES CASTLE
LEO CHALOUKIAN
CLIFFORD DEKTAR
DAN EINSTEIN
ROBERT S. FINKEL
DAVID E. FLUHR

RICHARD H. FRANK
GERIANN GERACI
DAN GINGOLD
SHERI GOLDBERG
JOHN E. GOLDHAMMER
DOUGLAS H. GRINDSTAFF
MICHAEL A. HOEY, A.C.E.
A. RICHARD LARSON
DARLENE LIEBLICH
LINDA J. LOE
MARGARET A. LOESCH
JAMES L. LOPER
SHEILA MANNING
BILL MILLAR

WILLIAM REINERT
MARY RICHARD
MARK ROSCH
JEFFREY B. ROSE
IRWIN ROSTEN
THOMAS W. SARNOFF
HANK D. SAROYAN
JAN SCOTT
SUSAN A. SIMONS
RICHARD STILES
GEORGE A. SUNGA
SY TOMASHOFF
MATHEW J. TOMBERS
MURRAY WEISSMAN
CHRISTOPHER W. WYATT

ANTI-SUBSTANCE ABUSE COMMITTEE

JOHN J. AGOGLIA
Chair

KERRY L. BROOM
RICHARD H. FRANK

LINDA MANCUSO
DEBORAH MILLER
THOMAS W. SARNOFF

MURRAY WEISSMAN

STAFF MEMBER: LINDA J. LOE

124

deceased

Very Special Thanks

To the distinguished professionals in the television industry who served on Emmy judging panels and gave freely of their time to screen and judge every nominated achievement.

To CBS, and especially to the executives of CBS Entertainment for their help in preparing The 1997 Primetime Emmy Awards *broadcast*.

To Ernst & Young for coordinating the voting tabulations and for other valued services.

To the American Federation of Television and Radio Artists, the Screen Actors Guild, the Directors Guild of America, the Writers Guild of America East and West, the American Federation of Musicians, and Theatre Authority West, Inc., for their cooperation.

To the contributors and suppliers of the ATAS institutional announcement: Clairmont Camera; Consolidated Film Industries; Eastman Kodak; Encore Video; The Post Group; Entertainment Partners; Alan Ett Music; Raintree Productions; Wollin Production Services; J.L. Fisher Productions; Hollywood Rental Co., Hector Elizondo; Coree Lear; Intelliprompt; Bob Romero, Mark Woods, Art Curtis; Michelle Otto; Mike Denecke; Dorrie Popovich; Red Sinclair; Brad Jarvis; Tim Merrill; Denny Clairmont; Jerry Virnig; Bob Mayson; Larry Chernoff; Rich Ellis; Dan Richter; Scott Liggett; Scott Wollin; Tony Finetti; Joe Finetti; Marry Matusz; Steve Redondo; Mike Bratkowski; Michael Graef; and Vahik Gregorian.

To everyone who contributed their time and continued support for the ATAS Foundation's Archive of American Television including, Janet S. Blake, Sue Chadwick, Sam Denoff, Tony Fantozzi, Morrie Gelman, Jeff Kisseloff, John Litvack, Leonard Maltin, Maxell Corporation of America, Kent McCray, Sandy Milred, Dan Pasternack, Tim Purnell, Grant A. Tinker, Dean Valentine, Bob Warren, David L. Wolper.

Special thanks to the individuals who have shared their incredible stories with the ATAS Foundation's Archive of American Television, which strives to be the most comprehensive account of television history: Joseph Barbera, Milton Berle, Haskell Boggs, Sid Caesar, Ralph Edwards, Elma Farnsworth, Ray Forrest, Les Flory, Leonard H. Goldenson, Don Hewitt, Loren Jones, Hal Kanter, Sheldon Leonard, Delbert Mann, Martin Manulis, JP Miller, Dick Smith, Nick Stewart, Betty White, Ethel Winant.

To the Public Relations Staff at CBS and especially Gil Schwartz, Chris Ender, Nancy Carr, Francis Cavanaugh, Joanna Massey, Emily Bear, Monty Brinton, Cliff Lipson, Sue Lamphear, Joyce Dortch and Stephanie Brice for providing and staffing the excellent media facilities.

To the Pasadena Police Department for coordinating the additional traffic occasioned by this event.

To the Pasadena Fire Department for coordinating public safety and fire protection facilities.

To the Pasadena Center staff for their excellent services — particularly to Roger Smith, CEO, Rick Barr, auditorium general manager, and Jess Waiters, vice president and executive director.

To Larson Sound Center for providing the venue for the sound mixing panels and to Audiotek Corp., Jeff Evans of Audio Intervisual Design, Steve Venezia and Karen Greshler of Dolby Labs and JBL Professional for their assistance in providing the equipment for the panels and Steve Potter and Tom Ancell for generously giving their time to run the panels.

To Mayor Rudolph Guiliani and the New York City Film Commission for their September 3rd reception honoring all New York area nominees.

To the Kodak Company for its September 6th dinner party honoring all cinematographer and lighting director nominees.

To the Kodak Company for providing Emmy winners with instant photos of their awards.

126 To the Directors Guild of America for its September 9th reception honoring all director nominees.

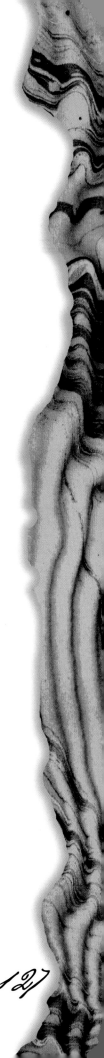

Very Special Thanks (cont'd.)

To the Screen Actors Guild, the American Federation of Television & Radio and Forever Spring for co-hosting with ATAS a September 10th reception honoring all performer nominees and past performer winners.

To Brian Gendese for his generous assistance on the September 10th Emmy Nominee party.

To the Writers Guild of America West for its September 12th reception honoring all writer nominees.

To Sherrie Lanese of the Beverly Hilton Hotel for her excellent assistance in organizing the Emmy Judging Panels.

To AVHQ and especially Pete Pandit for their valuable assistance in setting up and maintaining the video equipment used at the Emmy judging panels.

To all of the companies and individuals who contributed their time, energy and technology to making the Academy's World Wide Web Emmycast a huge success. To the EmmyCast '97 Ironlight team: Jason Oliver, Milanie Cleere, Jayson Tang, Rhonius Levi, Robert Bays, Ben Greenberg, Ann Haas, Julia Smith, Tobias Nownes, and Angie Nownes. Your time and dedication took this year's EmmyCast to a new level! To Henry Magallon and John Leverence from the Academy. To Yahoo! for the craziest promotion in online history, "Sign it and win the EmmyCast!" To E! Online for your chat engine and dedicated staff. To Kodak's Themed Entertainment Division for your ever so clear and sharp digital images. To Active Imaging. What would we do without these slick cameras? To The Ritz-Carlton, Huntington Hotel, the Official Hotel of EmmyCast '97. To President Tuxedo of San Francisco. To all EmmyCast '97 participants, especially Anthony Westreich, Ronald Wagner, Rebecca Shermerhorn, Ambrosia Dryden, Rachel Roth, Samantha Fein and Drena Rogers.

To Delicate Productions for lighting and sound.

To John Osborne for lighting design.

To Susan Tesh at VariLite for her generous donation.

To Merv Griffin Productions for event design and coordination.

To Patina's for catering.

To Regal Rents for rentals.

To Bob Dickinson and C. D. Simpson for lighting design – Creative Arts Awards.

To John Shaffner and Joe Stewart for set design – Creative Arts Awards.

To Evian Water for their generous water donation.

To Joel Groves and Valet Parking Services for coordinating Emmy parking.

To Pinkerton Security and Larry Jorgenson for security arrangements.

To Nancy Tokos for the Creative Arts Awards logo design.

To Scott Palazzo at Camera Ready Productions for additional production support on the Creative Arts Show.

To Dee Baker for production support on the Creative Arts Show.

To Craig Mathew for official photo coverage.

To Southern California Graphics for their assistance in the printing of the program.

To Penny Johnson for her work on the international Emmy spots.

Index to Advertisers

Photo Credits

Pages 14: Demi Moore, Cher and Sissy Spacek by Matthew Rolston/HBO. **Page 18**: Miss Evers' Boys by Bob Greene/HBO NYC. **Page 22**: Comedy Central Team by Bonnie Schiffman/HBO; Jac Venza by Nancy LeVine. **Page 30**: lan Arkin by Ron Tom/CBS; William H. Macy by Robert Ferrone/Shooting Star; Ewan McGregor by Paul Drinkwater/NBC. **Page 31**: Craig Mathew. **Page 39**: Anne Meara by David M. Spindel; sabella Rossellini by Spike Nannarello/CBS. **Page 48**: Mel Brooks by Paul Drinkwater/NBC; James Earl Jones by Gale M. Adler/NBC; Jerry Stiller by David M. Spindel. **Page 66**: Carol Burnett by Paul Drinkwater/NBC; Marsha Mason by Firooz Zahedi. **Page 72**: Craig Mathew. **Page 74**: Bryant Gumbel by Tony Esparza/CBS. **Page 81**: Jason Alexander by Chris Haston; David Hyde Pierce by Chris Haston; Michael Richards by Gwendolen Cates/SYGMA; Rip Torn by Darryl Estrine/HBO. **Page 83**: Janeane Garofalo by Larry Watson/HBO; Kristen Johnston by Alan Levenson; Lisa Kudrow by Chris Haston. **Page 86**: Bette Midler by Greg Gorman/HBO. **Page 87**: CCH Pounder by Robert Hale; Della Reese by Cliff Lipson. **Page 88**: Adam Arkin by Kevin Merrill/Shooting Star; Eriq LaSalle by Chris Haston; Nicholas Turturro by Timothy White/ABC. **Page 89**: Beau Bridges by Rafy; Michael Caine by Kelvin Jones; Ossie Davis by Bob Greene/HBO. **Page 90**: Kirstie Alley by Chris Haston; Bridget Fonda by Ken Regan/HBO NYC; Glenne Headly by Erik Heinila; Frances McDormand by Rafy; Diana Rigg by Sophie Baker/Carlton UK. **Page 96**: Beau Bridges by Rafy; Laurence Fishburne by Jeff Katz; Sidney Poitier by Kevin Jones. **Page 98**: Stockard Channing by Joe Lederer; Glenn Close by Ken Regan/HBO NY; Helen Mirren by Bob Greene/HBO; Meryl Streep by Andrew Eccles/ABC; Alfre Woodard by Alex Baile. **Page 100**: Fran Drescher by Spike Nanarello; Helen Hunt by Chris Haston; Patricia Richardson by Wayne Stambler/CPi. **Page 101**: Michael J. Fox by George Lange/ABC; John Lithgow by Alan Levenson/NBC. **Page 102**: Roma Downey by Cliff Lipson/CBS; Christine Lahti by Cliff Lipson/CBS; Julianna Margulies by Chris Haston/NBC; Sherry Stringfield by Paul Drinkwater. **Page 103**: Smits by Gwendolyn Cates; Sam Waterston by James Sorensen. **Page 114-16**: Craig Mathew.